بسم الله الرحمن الرحيم

English Edition published in May 2005
Reprinted in July 2009

Published by:
Ta-Ha Publishers Ltd.
Unit 4, The Windsor Centre
Windsor Grove
West Norwood
London, SE27 9NT
United Kingdom

Website: http://www.taha.co.uk
E-Mail: sales @ taha.co.uk

By Adem Yakup
Translated By: Ron Evans
Edited By: Abdassamad Clarke

ISBN 978 1 84200 068 7

Printed and bound by:
Secil Ofset in İstanbul
Address: Yüzyıl Mahallesi MAS-SIT Matbaacılar Sitesi
4. Cadde No:77 Bağcılar- İstanbul / TURKEY

Website: http: // www.ademyakup.com

Ta-Ha Publishers Ltd.
Unit 4, The Windsor Centre Windsor Grove West Norwood
London, SE27 9NT United Kingdom

JANNAH
The Garden from the Qur'an and Hadith

Whereas those who have iman and
do right actions, such people
are the Companions of the Garden,
remaining in it timelessly, for ever.
(Surat al-Baqara: 82)

ADEM YAKUP

Contents

Introduction

In the life of this world, human beings are responsible for overcoming the impulses and appetites of their *nafs* (selves) and living their lives to please Allah. To do this we have been given a very short lifespan of sixty or seventy years on average. After the life of this world is over, Allah has created an endless and perfect life for His slaves who have won His favour. In comparison to that timeless existence, life in this world lasts only as long as the blink of an eye. The faithful slaves are those who have shown steadfastness and determination in living according to the genuine knowledge of the unity of Allah without association of partners to Him and in obedience to Allah and His Messenger ﷺ. They will obtain a great reward in the world to come: the eternal life of the Garden. Doubtless the favour, mercy and love of our Lord for His slaves are a great joy for them.

Allah has created each person with a spirit that takes pleasure in and yearns for the best and finest things in life, because those beautiful things reflect the wonders of the Garden in the Unseen. From the first moment that someone has begun to understand the meaning of life, a person feels a constant desire to attain perfection. He is always in search of the blessings that this life has to offer. But no matter how strong his desire and no matter how hard he works to attain these good things, he will never find the perfection he is looking for in the world. This is because Allah has created the life of this world imperfect and unfulfilling.

There are many reasons why Allah has created the world in this way. As Allah tells us in the Qur'an, His creation is flawless. **"He is Allah – the Creator, the Maker, the Giver of Form. To Him belong the Most Beautiful Names. Everything in the heavens and earth glorifies Him. He is the Almighty, the All-Wise."** (Surat al-Hashr: 24) Our Lord's power is infinite and He can create what He wants. Therefore, there is a purpose in the defects of the world: Allah wants people to know that the Garden exists and to work towards it with eagerness and sincerity.

Allah has created human character such that we can only be at ease in the Garden and the desires of the heart can only be fulfilled there. Many verses of the Qur'an make this clear. Allah says in it that the real life is the life of the Garden and, therefore, every effort should be expended to attain this abode of endless good and beauty. Some verses of the Qur'an on this subject are as follows:

> **The life of this world is nothing but a game and a diversion. The abode of the akhira – that is truly Life if they only knew. (Surat al-'Ankabut: 64)**

> **The truly good will be in perfect bliss on couches gazing in wonder. You will recognise in their faces the radiance of delight. They are given the choicest sealed wine to drink, whose seal is musk – let people with aspiration aspire to that! (Surat al-Mutaffifin: 22-26)**

> **Allah expands provision to anyone He wills and restricts it. They rejoice in the life of this world. Yet the life of this world, compared**

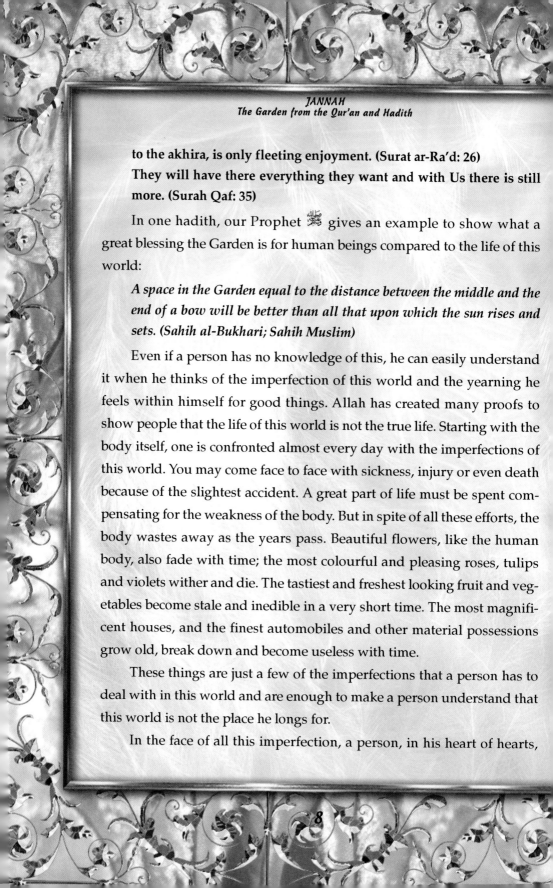

to the akhira, is only fleeting enjoyment. **(Surat ar-Ra'd: 26)**
**They will have there everything they want and with Us there is still
more. (Surah Qaf: 35)**

In one hadith, our Prophet gives an example to show what a
great blessing the Garden is for human beings compared to the life of this
world:

*A space in the Garden equal to the distance between the middle and the
end of a bow will be better than all that upon which the sun rises and
sets. (Sahih al-Bukhari; Sahih Muslim)*

Even if a person has no knowledge of this, he can easily understand
it when he thinks of the imperfection of this world and the yearning he
feels within himself for good things. Allah has created many proofs to
show people that the life of this world is not the true life. Starting with the
body itself, one is confronted almost every day with the imperfections of
this world. You may come face to face with sickness, injury or even death
because of the slightest accident. A great part of life must be spent com-
pensating for the weakness of the body. But in spite of all these efforts, the
body wastes away as the years pass. Beautiful flowers, like the human
body, also fade with time; the most colourful and pleasing roses, tulips
and violets wither and die. The tastiest and freshest looking fruit and veg-
etables become stale and inedible in a very short time. The most magnificent houses, and the finest automobiles and other material possessions
grow old, break down and become useless with time.

These things are just a few of the imperfections that a person has to
deal with in this world and are enough to make a person understand that
this world is not the place he longs for.

In the face of all this imperfection, a person, in his heart of hearts,

Race each other to forgiveness from
your Lord and a Garden as wide as the
heavens and the earth, prepared for the
people who have taqwa.
(Surah Al 'Imran: 133)

wants to live in a world where perfection is never-ending. He longs for a world where there is no illness, death, war, conflict, evil, anxiety or imperfection. With this in mind, he looks for ways to establish a life within the parameters of this world that is happy and carefree. However, Allah tells us in the Qur'an that this kind of life can only be had in the Garden. What human beings must do to attain the Garden is very simple: live in a way that is pleasing to Allah. Then, if Allah wills, they will find a perfect and endless life happy beyond all that they could desire or imagine.

Allah says much in the Qur'an about the blessings of the Garden because He wants people to understand that everything they are looking for, longing for and everything they love is in the Garden. In the following chapters of this book we will look at verses of the Qur'an and hadith of our Prophet ﷺ to see the perfect blessings that our Lord has prepared for us.

One of the purposes of this book is to remind people that the real life is not in this world, but in the Garden, and what our hearts desire is not here but there. Even if you have never considered it before, this book will help you to understand that the longing you feel for perfection can only be fulfilled in the life of the Garden.

Another purpose of this book is to move our readers to consider the incomparable beauty of the Garden and the never-ending pleasure that will be the believers'. The verses of the Qur'an and the hadith of our Prophet ﷺ tell us about blessings of the Garden that many people have perhaps never thought about before. An understanding of the splendour of the Garden, its limitless blessings and the good life that will be lived there will increase people's longing for the Garden and make us strive harder to attain it. This book may be a means to help people take pleasure in their resolve to do such good works that they may be worthy of Allah's endless mercy and His incomparable blessings.

Of course, our capacity to grasp the descriptions of the Garden throughout this book are limited by the limitations of the human mind. Indeed, the perfection and beauty announced by Allah in the Qur'an and described in the hadith of our Prophet 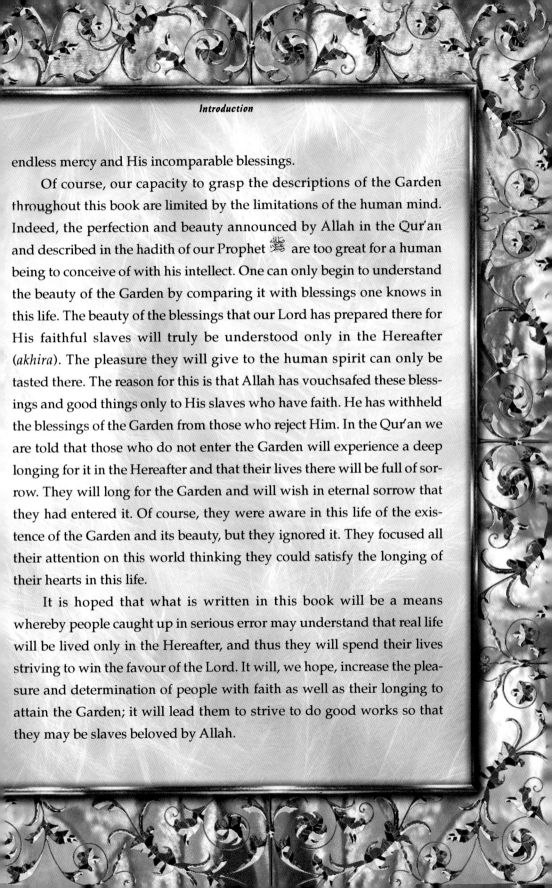 are too great for a human being to conceive of with his intellect. One can only begin to understand the beauty of the Garden by comparing it with blessings one knows in this life. The beauty of the blessings that our Lord has prepared there for His faithful slaves will truly be understood only in the Hereafter (*akhira*). The pleasure they will give to the human spirit can only be tasted there. The reason for this is that Allah has vouchsafed these blessings and good things only to His slaves who have faith. He has withheld the blessings of the Garden from those who reject Him. In the Qur'an we are told that those who do not enter the Garden will experience a deep longing for it in the Hereafter and that their lives there will be full of sorrow. They will long for the Garden and will wish in eternal sorrow that they had entered it. Of course, they were aware in this life of the existence of the Garden and its beauty, but they ignored it. They focused all their attention on this world thinking they could satisfy the longing of their hearts in this life.

It is hoped that what is written in this book will be a means whereby people caught up in serious error may understand that real life will be lived only in the Hereafter, and thus they will spend their lives striving to win the favour of the Lord. It will, we hope, increase the pleasure and determination of people with faith as well as their longing to attain the Garden; it will lead them to strive to do good works so that they may be slaves beloved by Allah.

The Blessings Allah Has Prepared for the People of the Garden

*S*ometimes films have been made and novels written about things people wish for but which are impossible to obtain because of the way the world is. These things are thought to be fantastic or utopian and beyond the realm of reality. Many people long for these imaginary perfections and want them to be real. But knowing that these wonderful things cannot happen in the real world and that they exist only in the imagination, people do not form a deep longing for them in their spirits. On the contrary, they become even more aware of the imperfections that surround them; they see the world's real face, which makes them "feel depressed." Of course, only people without faith get caught up in this state.

Those who believe with certainty in the existence of the Hereafter know that all possibilities that stretch the boundaries of the imagination can come to be by Allah's command and that they will attain the blessing of the Garden in the Hereafter. This being the case, a person may hope to attain in the Garden all the blessings he would like to have had on Earth. With this hope, a person will exert himself seriously to be worthy of the Garden where he will be granted everything he desires.

Our Prophet 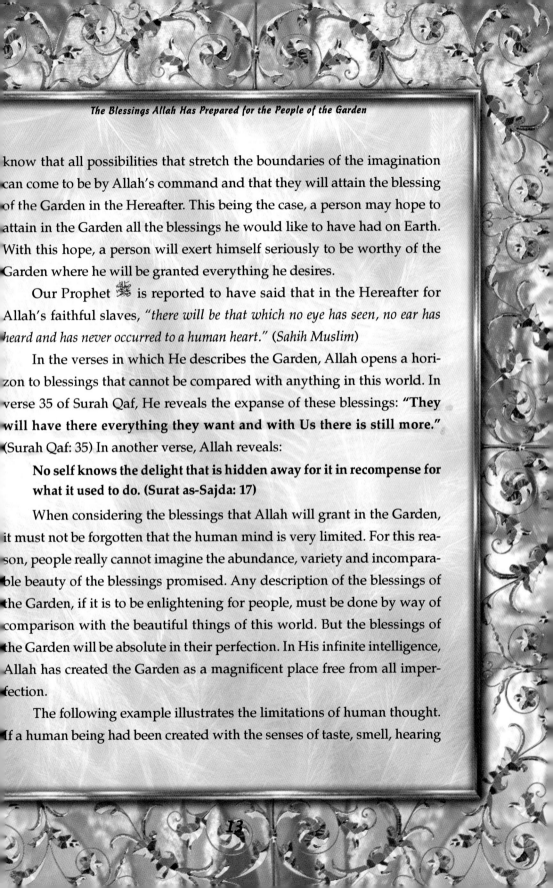 is reported to have said that in the Hereafter for Allah's faithful slaves, *"there will be that which no eye has seen, no ear has heard and has never occurred to a human heart."* (Sahih Muslim)

In the verses in which He describes the Garden, Allah opens a horizon to blessings that cannot be compared with anything in this world. In verse 35 of Surah Qaf, He reveals the expanse of these blessings: **"They will have there everything they want and with Us there is still more."** (Surah Qaf: 35) In another verse, Allah reveals:

No self knows the delight that is hidden away for it in recompense for what it used to do. (Surat as-Sajda: 17)

When considering the blessings that Allah will grant in the Garden, it must not be forgotten that the human mind is very limited. For this reason, people really cannot imagine the abundance, variety and incomparable beauty of the blessings promised. Any description of the blessings of the Garden, if it is to be enlightening for people, must be done by way of comparison with the beautiful things of this world. But the blessings of the Garden will be absolute in their perfection. In His infinite intelligence, Allah has created the Garden as a magnificent place free from all imperfection.

The following example illustrates the limitations of human thought. If a human being had been created with the senses of taste, smell, hearing and touch but without the sense of sight, he would never have been able to conceive of visual beauty no matter how much it was described to him. He would never be able to understand when people spoke to him of colour, daylight, proportion, symmetry or visual splendours. By the same token, there may be other senses that we know nothing about at present, but which Allah will create in the Garden to give us a totally new outlook. Therefore, in this world where we are limited to five senses, we cannot imagine what kind of blessings there may be that may be beyond our ability to conceive.

With our limitations of sight, thought and imagination, we are like people in a windowless house who never come out. Such people are unaware of the beautiful things outside the house – mountains, rivers, trees, beautiful flowers, animals, clear skies, bright sun-lit days – and so cannot be aware that they live deprived of many blessings. In addition, the comparison we make is based on the good things of this world. The blessings of this world are extremely lacking when compared with the blessings of the Garden and a person of faith must avoid the error of interpreting even the limited things he knows about the Garden from a narrow viewpoint. Apart from the things our Lord has revealed about the Garden, a person has no idea of what surprises have been prepared for the people of the Garden. Here is one of the verses of the Qur'an that tells us about this: **"They will have there everything they want and with Us there is still more."** (Surah Qaf: 35)

It is said that our Prophet ﷺ described the blessings of the Garden in these words:

> *Isn't there anybody hastening to the Garden? Because in the Garden there are unimaginable blessings. (Mukhtasar at-Tadhkirah, al-Qurtubi, pp. 306-307/499)*

Their Lord gives them
the good news
of His mercy and
good pleasure and
Gardens where
they will enjoy
everlasting delight.
(Surat at-Tawba: 21)

The Abundant Wealth of the Garden

In non-religious societies, wealth has always been the symbol of power and respect and it has been among the major goals that people strive for throughout their lives. One of the reasons for this is that people without faith believe that they will only be truly happy if they are wealthy. They think that they can only secure their possessions and achieve comfort, ease and the beautiful things they like in this way. For this reason, they spend their whole lives amassing property and possessions, saving money and making the right investments. They worry that their possessions will be used up and so they do not make use of them, they avoid spending money at all costs and do everything they can to preserve their wealth.

But in the life of this world, a person's wealth will not bring him the pleasure he expects no matter how hard he works for it. It may give him comfort in some ways, but in this flawed and imperfect world wealth is also flawed and imperfect. The Arabic word *dunya* (world) is derived from the word *dani* which means "low, inferior, simple, worthless."

A reason why Allah created the world flawed, and as a transitory place is to allow people to appreciate better the good things of the Garden. For example, if a person who has lived in poverty since childhood is invited to a home with magnificent furniture and priceless works of art, decorated with precious stones, and is offered rare foods to eat, he would be struck by the beauty of the place. Doubtless, this person's delight would be much greater than that of someone who has lived in such an environment since childhood. Our position in this world is similar to that of a person brought up in poverty and want. But even the world's wealthiest person is poor in comparison to the riches of the Garden. And, in this world, a person can never attain this true wealth. Even the richest person in the world will finally be wrapped in a few metres of cloth or put into a coffin and buried in the ground, leaving all his wealth behind. Allah tells us in the Qur'an that the blessings of the world are transitory:

> **The metaphor of the life of the world is that of water which We send down from the sky, and which then mingles with the plants of the earth to provide food for both people and animals. Then, when the earth is at its loveliest and takes on its fairest guise and its people think they have it under their control, Our command comes upon it by night or day and We reduce it to dried-out stubble, as though it had not been flourishing just the day before! In this way We make Our Signs clear for people who reflect. (Surah Yunus: 24)**

The wealth of the Garden, unlike the wealth of this world, is an everlasting wealth that people will experience in their hearts and with their bodies and senses, without worrying that it will ever come to an end. This verse in the Qur'an tells us about the beautiful wealth of the Garden: **"Seeing them, you see delight and a great kingdom."** (Surat al-Insan: 20)

The wealth of the Garden is a harmony containing the artistry of Allah's endless bounty and dazzling splendour. All of this beauty is presented in such a way as to fulfil the believers' passions and desires, because it is only when wealth is turned into beauty in this way that it can give meaning to the human spirit.

In the following pages several hadith are included illustrating how beautiful it is to dwell in the Garden and we will describe its wealth at the same time. The beauty of these places, apart from their aesthetic qualities, comes from the value of the materials used to decorate them. In a hadith, our Prophet ﷺ replied to someone who asked about what materials the Garden is built from:

> *One brick of gold and one brick of silver, its mortar is of strongly scented musk, its stones are pearls and emeralds, and its soil is of saffron ... (Narrated by Abu Hurayra, at-Tirmidhi)*

The wealth promised to the people of the Garden is limitless; it is in abundance, and there is no worry that it will ever be used up.

The Treasures of the Garden:

These treasures mentioned earlier in the hadith emphasise the splendour of the Garden. When thinking about this, we should remember that it is a creation of Allah Whose possessions are limitless and He gives them to those of His slaves whom He wills. And in case we think of those treasures in entirely material terms, our Prophet ﷺ reminds us in these words:

> *"Shall I not guide you to one of the treasures of the Garden?" I said: "Yes, Messenger of Allah!" Thereupon he 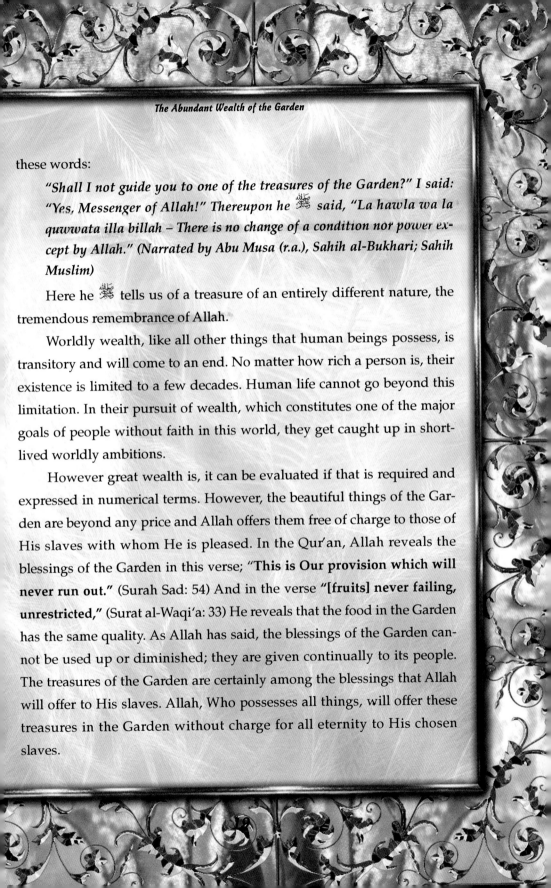 said, "La hawla wa la quwwata illa billah – There is no change of a condition nor power except by Allah." (Narrated by Abu Musa (r.a.), Sahih al-Bukhari; Sahih Muslim)*

Here he 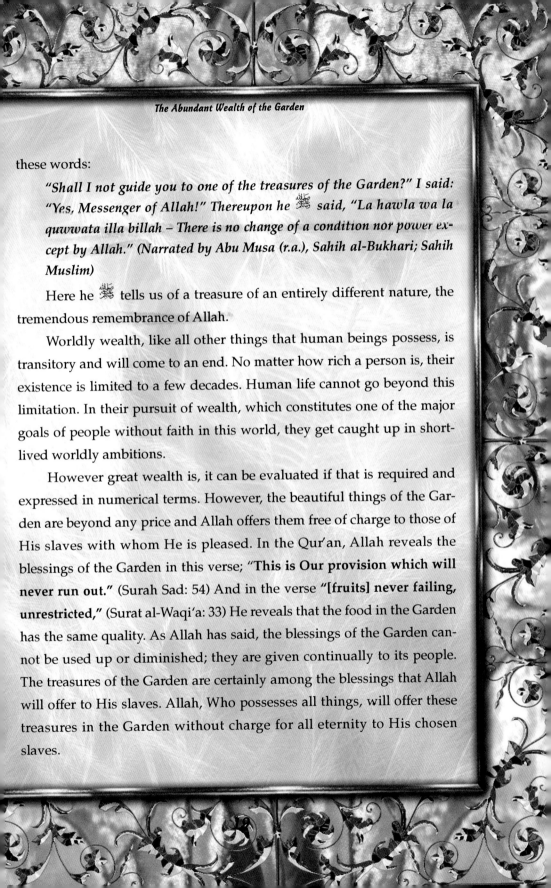 tells us of a treasure of an entirely different nature, the tremendous remembrance of Allah.

Worldly wealth, like all other things that human beings possess, is transitory and will come to an end. No matter how rich a person is, their existence is limited to a few decades. Human life cannot go beyond this limitation. In their pursuit of wealth, which constitutes one of the major goals of people without faith in this world, they get caught up in short-lived worldly ambitions.

However great wealth is, it can be evaluated if that is required and expressed in numerical terms. However, the beautiful things of the Garden are beyond any price and Allah offers them free of charge to those of His slaves with whom He is pleased. In the Qur'an, Allah reveals the blessings of the Garden in this verse; **"This is Our provision which will never run out."** (Surah Sad: 54) And in the verse **"[fruits] never failing, unrestricted,"** (Surat al-Waqi'a: 33) He reveals that the food in the Garden has the same quality. As Allah has said, the blessings of the Garden cannot be used up or diminished; they are given continually to its people. The treasures of the Garden are certainly among the blessings that Allah will offer to His slaves. Allah, Who possesses all things, will offer these treasures in the Garden without charge for all eternity to His chosen slaves.

The Abundance of Possessions in the Garden:

In the Garden, wealth and possessions are abundant and free. Our Prophet ﷺ says the following about the abundance of the Garden:

The one with the lowest rank from among the inhabitants of the Garden will be that person who will be able to see his gardens, wives, luxuries, servants and things of enjoyment to the distance of one thousand years... (Narrated by Ibn Umar, at-Tirmidhi)

If as much of what is in the Garden as could be carried by a fingernail were to appear, the space between the cardinal points of the heavens and the earth would be adorned on account of it. If a man of the inhabitants of the Garden were to look down and his bracelets were to appear, his light would obliterate the light of the sun just as the sun obliterates the light of the stars. (Narrated by Sa'd ibn Abi Waqqas, at-Tirmidhi)

As these hadith point out, even a small portion of the blessings of the Garden is enormous when measured according to worldly standards. This abundance is emphasised in one of the above hadith when he ﷺ says that the bracelets are more brilliant than the sun.

Precious Stones and Metals

In the Qur'an, Allah reveals that there are luxurious items, various jewels and precious stones in the Garden. "**[They are] on sumptuous woven couches**" (Surat al-Wa'qia: 15) and "**They will enter Gardens of Eden where they will be adorned with gold bracelets and pearls.**" (Surah Fatir: 33) These jewels that are mentioned in the Qur'an and in the hadith in relation to the Garden have been expressions throughout human history of wealth and splendour. Everyone appreciates these adornments of diamonds, pearls, rubies, gold and silver, and takes pleasure in seeing things decorated with them.

There are some hadith, such as those below that mention pearls as a blessing of the Garden:

Those who dwell in the Garden of Eternity will wear crowns encrusted with pearls, the radiance of the smallest of which will illuminate the space separating the east from the west! (At-Tirmidhi)

'Abd-Allah ibn 'Amr said: "I heard the Messenger of Allah ﷺ saying that the [Yemeni] Corner and the Station [of Ibrahim] are two of the precious stones of the Garden, whose light has been extinguished by Allah. If He had not extinguished their light, it would illuminate everything between the east and the west." (At-Tirmidhi, 804)

Pearls are a good example of the rare value of the blessings of the Garden. Divers must go down several times into the dangerous depths of the sea to bring them up, and this adornment is found in only a few of the many oysters that are collected. Besides its beauty, what gives value to this little object is, as we said above, the effort required to obtain it and its great rarity.

Much time, effort and expense is required in this world to obtain the pearl, but they are abundant in the world to come. The fact that such a rare and valuable object of beauty is plentiful will doubtless produce a particular excitement in the human spirit. Moreover, the blessings of the Garden revealed in the Qur'an will have a beauty that is beyond our capacity to imagine. The hadith mention a pearl that illuminates everything between East and West, but we cannot completely picture the brilliance and splendour of such a pearl in our minds.

The Beauty of the Dwellings of the Garden

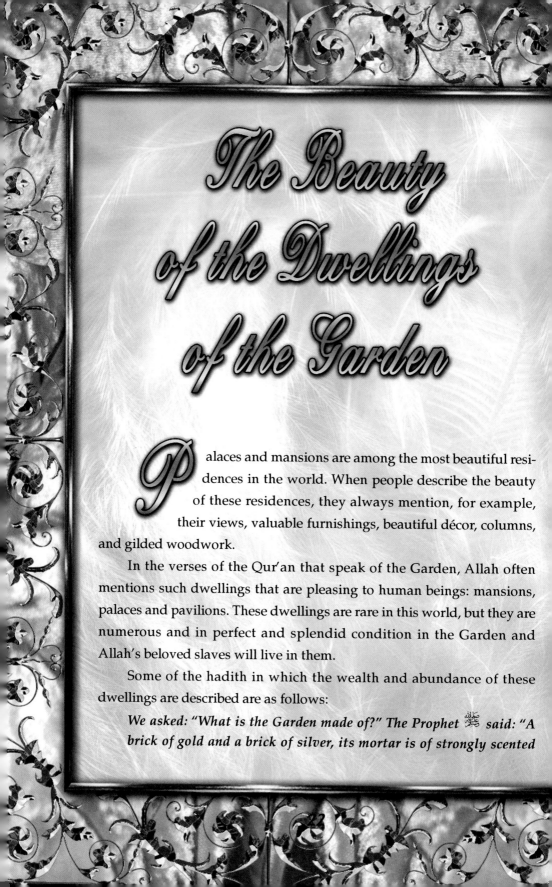

Palaces and mansions are among the most beautiful residences in the world. When people describe the beauty of these residences, they always mention, for example, their views, valuable furnishings, beautiful décor, columns, and gilded woodwork.

In the verses of the Qur'an that speak of the Garden, Allah often mentions such dwellings that are pleasing to human beings: mansions, palaces and pavilions. These dwellings are rare in this world, but they are numerous and in perfect and splendid condition in the Garden and Allah's beloved slaves will live in them.

Some of the hadith in which the wealth and abundance of these dwellings are described are as follows:

We asked: "What is the Garden made of?" The Prophet said: "A brick of gold and a brick of silver, its mortar is of strongly scented

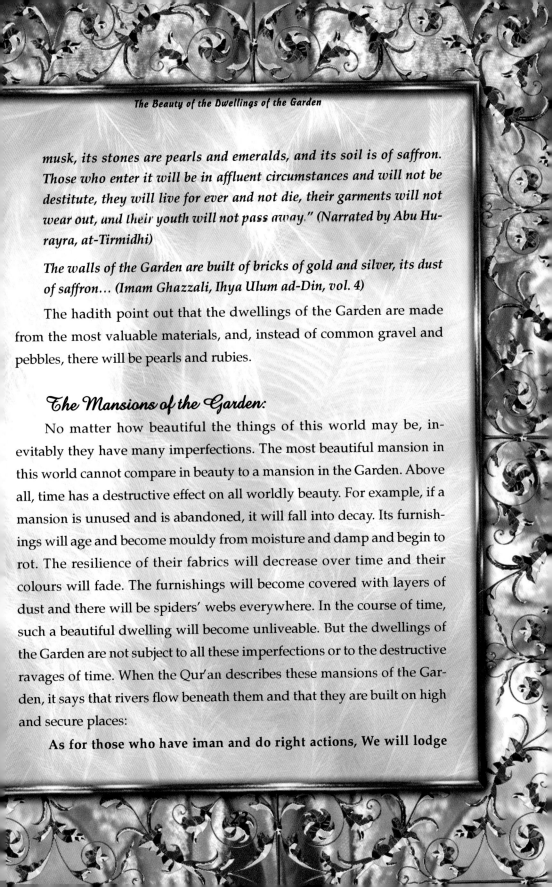

musk, its stones are pearls and emeralds, and its soil is of saffron. Those who enter it will be in affluent circumstances and will not be destitute, they will live for ever and not die, their garments will not wear out, and their youth will not pass away." (Narrated by Abu Hurayra, at-Tirmidhi)

The walls of the Garden are built of bricks of gold and silver, its dust of saffron... (Imam Ghazzali, Ihya Ulum ad-Din, vol. 4)

The hadith point out that the dwellings of the Garden are made from the most valuable materials, and, instead of common gravel and pebbles, there will be pearls and rubies.

The Mansions of the Garden:

No matter how beautiful the things of this world may be, inevitably they have many imperfections. The most beautiful mansion in this world cannot compare in beauty to a mansion in the Garden. Above all, time has a destructive effect on all worldly beauty. For example, if a mansion is unused and is abandoned, it will fall into decay. Its furnishings will age and become mouldy from moisture and damp and begin to rot. The resilience of their fabrics will decrease over time and their colours will fade. The furnishings will become covered with layers of dust and there will be spiders' webs everywhere. In the course of time, such a beautiful dwelling will become unliveable. But the dwellings of the Garden are not subject to all these imperfections or to the destructive ravages of time. When the Qur'an describes these mansions of the Garden, it says that rivers flow beneath them and that they are built on high and secure places:

As for those who have iman and do right actions, We will lodge

them in lofty chambers in the Garden, with rivers flowing under them, remaining in them timelessly, for ever. How excellent is the reward of those who act. (Surat al-'Ankabut: 58)

It is not your wealth or your children that will bring you near to Us – only in the case of people who have iman and act rightly; such people will have a double recompense for what they did. They will be safe from all harm in the High Halls of the Garden. (Surah Saba': 37)

Every detail in the description of the Garden speaks to every period of time and appeals to everyone. Rubies, emeralds, pearls and other precious stones are rare and valuable and everyone appreciates them. For this reason, that the mansions are made of these stones is an important indication of their priceless value.

Among these stones, the reddish transparent ruby is the rarest precious stone in the world. The shiny, smooth, round pearl has an extraordinary aesthetic beauty. Its formation is very special. Over time, a little grain of sand inside an oyster irritates the soft inward of the oyster which covers it with calcium carbonate until it eventually becomes a thing of striking beauty. Of course, these descriptions and comparisons with regard to the Garden are examples taken from the conditions pertaining in this world. These comparisons are necessary as a means to broaden our horizons and for us to think about the Garden. But the beautiful things of the Garden will be much more magnificent than the jewels of this world.

Everything in the Garden has been created to be as pleasant as possible. The Prophet ﷺ says the following about the mansions in the Garden:

In the garden there is a tent of pearls, whose width is sixty miles, in each corner of which the believer will have a wife whom the others will not see. (Sahih al-Bukhari)

Another thing that adds to the beauty of these mansions is the splen-

Gardens of Eden with rivers flowing
under them, remaining in them
timelessly, for ever. That is the reward
of those who purify themselves.
(Surah Ta Ha: 76)

did setting in which they are located. For example, as we see in many descriptions, some mansions are surrounded by greenery and stand over or near water.

In addition, there is another characteristic of these mansions in the Garden:

There are mansions made of emeralds and jewels. (Imam Ghazzali, Ihya Ulum ad-Din [The Revival of the Sciences of the Deen], vol. 4)

Everything has been created in the Garden according to what people desire and nothing they wish to see is withheld from their eyes. Allah reveals this in the Qur'an:

... They will have there all that their hearts desire and their eyes find delight in... (Surat az-Zukhruf: 71)

Cities in the Garden:

There is a river known as "Rayyan" in the Garden. A city of coral has been built upon it. It has seventy thousand gates of gold and silver. (Ahmad Diya ad-Din al-Kamushkhanawi, Ramuz al-Ahadith, vol. 2, p. 326/4)

In the above hadith, our Prophet ﷺ tells of gold and silver, the symbols of splendid wealth and art. Because both these metals are brilliant, resilient, easy to shape and difficult to find they have held an important place throughout history. There is only as much as 0.004 grams of gold in a ton of earth; the amount per ton obtained in gold mines, however, varies between 6 and 12 grams. Therefore, to obtain a gold plate, tons of rocks must be refined. The fact that gold is hard to obtain and is rarer than other metals in the world increases its value greatly. And this shiny, resilient and easy to shape metal has also a strong aesthetic appeal to people.

The aesthetic and artistic value of gold makes it the metal of choice in the production of fine works of art. Many of the things we find rich and extravagant are either made of gold or decorated with it. In the adornment of objects, in bookbinding, calligraphy, miniatures and illumination, gold is indispensable. The lavish use of gold in the dwellings described in the hadith is a blessing that people find pleasing. In this world, people see gold often in the form of ingots; once in a while they come across a few gold-plated objects and accessories and perhaps even palaces with excessive use of gold such as in gilt columns. All these things are amazing to those of us who are accustomed to seeing only a few pieces of jewellery made of gold. This being the case, we cannot easily imagine a skyscraper or a mansion, a villa or a summer house made purely of gold. Just the idea that there may be such things gives pleasure and excitement to the human spirit. The hadith we have quoted previously tells us that the buildings in the Garden are made of gold and silver bricks. This increases the beauty of the already splendid houses in the Garden and makes them even more magnificent.

> *[It is built of] one brick of gold and one brick of silver, its mortar is of strongly scented musk, its stones are pearls and emeralds, and its soil is of saffron... (Narrated by Abu Hurayra, at-Tirmidhi)*

In the hadith below, another aspect of the splendour of the Garden is emphasised by reference to a gold pillar:

> *In the Garden there is a gold pillar with cities of beryl [a bright, green precious stone resembling emerald] on it, and these shine like stars in the Garden... (Ahmad Diya ad-Din al-Kamushkhanawi, Ramuz al-Ahadith, vol. 1, p. 125/6)*

Another interesting aspect of the above hadith is the high elevation of the cities. Certainly in this world a highly elevated city is to be preferred because of the view and refreshing climate. When we consider that these cities are in the splendid setting of the Garden, we can better understand to what extent these dwellings will be pleasing to the human spirit. These dwellings spoken of in the hadith – cities on pillars – have a parallel in the verses of the Qur'an that tell us about high-ceilinged halls built one above the other:

> **But those who have taqwa of their Lord will have high-ceilinged Halls, and more such Halls built one above the other, and rivers flowing under them. That is Allah's promise. Allah does not break His promise. (Surat az-Zumar: 20)**

When we think of life in a city, first of all, many problems come to mind. Traffic, health, communication, air pollution, infrastructure, water, electricity, telephones and security have become matters that people have to struggle with. Many professions have even come into existence to mitigate these problems and help people lead more untroubled and ordered lives. The reasons for such problems will be eradicated in the Garden and there is no possibility that such conditions could ever exist in the cities there.

The Qur'an tells us that the climate of the Garden will be the most pleasant and comfortable for the human spirit: "**...they will experience there neither burning sun nor bitter cold.**" (Surat al-Insan: 13) For this reason, there will be no need for heating systems or air conditioning. As we will see in the following chapters, communication will be no problem in the Garden. Allah knows the truth.

When the buildings of the Garden are mentioned in the hadith, the Prophet ﷺ says that their mortar will be a sweet-smelling material called musk. We can see that all the blessings that Allah has created in the Garden appeal to all our senses. A sweet aroma is a wonderful blessing for human beings. The scent of roses, carnations, lilies, hyacinths, lilacs, acacia and pine trees are all gifts of Allah to human beings. In addition, these wonderful smells have a pleasing effect on the human spirit. Nothing in this world will be able to compare with the aromas of the Garden and people will enjoy all their unexpected subtleties. The fact that the mortar of the buildings is composed of musk is one of the best examples of this. This is only one of the wonderful things that Allah has created for believers in the Garden.

The Palaces of the Garden:

In one hadith, the palaces of the Garden are mentioned:

In the Garden, there are palaces built of emeralds and jewels and in each building there will be 70 rooms of red colour and in each room 70 sub-rooms of green colour and in each sub-room there will be one throne... There will be 70 dining cloths in each room and 70 kinds of food on each dining cloth. There will be seven servants in each room... (Imam Ghazzali, Ihya Ulum ad-Din, vol. 4)

We are told that the palaces of the Garden are made of the most precious stones, that they are decorated in the most beautiful and pleasing manner and that they are full of blessings. Believers who are not content with the life of this world and who are not deceived by the attractions of this transitory world will be blessed in the Hereafter with real gifts that are perfect and everlasting. Because they have had a pure iman, and have willingly made serious effort toward the attainment of the Garden, they will have true delight forever in its beautiful

But as for those who have iman
and do right actions, We will
admit them into Gardens
with rivers flowing under them,
remaining in them timelessly,
for ever and ever.
Allah's promise is true.
Whose speech could
be truer than Allah's?
(Surat an-Nisa': 122)

dwellings. As well as containing every luxury and splendid wealth, this environment will be a pure and noble place where the people of the Garden always remember Allah and give Him heartfelt thanks. In the Qur'an, Allah tells us that the people of the Garden live there in continual thankfulness and happiness:

> **They will say, "Praise be to Allah Who has fulfilled His promise to us and made us the inheritors of this land, letting us settle in the Garden wherever we want. How excellent is the wage of those who work!" (Surat az-Zumar: 74)**

The Cool Pavilions of the Garden:

Many hadith describe the tents that are among the dwellings of the Garden. Some of these hadith are as follows:

> *A tent [in the Garden] is like a hollow pearl, thirty miles in height and in every corner of the tent, a believer will have a wife who cannot be seen by the others. (Narrated by Abu Musa al-Ash'ari; Sahih al-Bukhari, vol. 4, hadith no: 466)*

> *In the Garden the believer will have a tent made of a single hollow pearl, whose width will be sixty miles. The believer will have wives in it, and he will go to each of them without any of them seeing each other. (Narrated by Abu Bakr ibn Abdullah ibn Qais, Sahih Muslim, vol. 4, hadith no: 2838)*

> *The least of the people of the Garden in rank is the one who will have eighty thousand servants and seventy two wives, and for whom will be set up a dome of pearls, aquamarine and rubies similar in dimensions to the distance between Jabiyah and San'a. (Abu Sa'id al-Khudri, at-Tirmidhi)*

> *[In the Garden] a tent of pearls, emeralds and jewels will be pitched*

for the believer. (Sunan Ibn Majah, at-Tirmidhi)

Everything in the Garden has been created in the most perfect way and the pavilions are as comfortable as possible to give pleasure, comfort and relaxation to believers. The Messenger of Allah 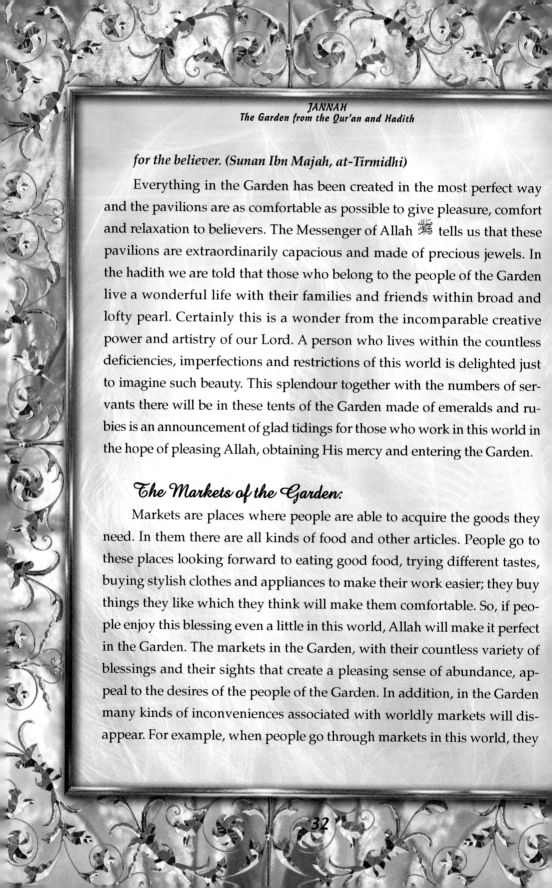 tells us that these pavilions are extraordinarily capacious and made of precious jewels. In the hadith we are told that those who belong to the people of the Garden live a wonderful life with their families and friends within broad and lofty pearl. Certainly this is a wonder from the incomparable creative power and artistry of our Lord. A person who lives within the countless deficiencies, imperfections and restrictions of this world is delighted just to imagine such beauty. This splendour together with the numbers of servants there will be in these tents of the Garden made of emeralds and rubies is an announcement of glad tidings for those who work in this world in the hope of pleasing Allah, obtaining His mercy and entering the Garden.

The Markets of the Garden:

Markets are places where people are able to acquire the goods they need. In them there are all kinds of food and other articles. People go to these places looking forward to eating good food, trying different tastes, buying stylish clothes and appliances to make their work easier; they buy things they like which they think will make them comfortable. So, if people enjoy this blessing even a little in this world, Allah will make it perfect in the Garden. The markets in the Garden, with their countless variety of blessings and their sights that create a pleasing sense of abundance, appeal to the desires of the people of the Garden. In addition, in the Garden many kinds of inconveniences associated with worldly markets will disappear. For example, when people go through markets in this world, they quickly become weary even though they enjoy themselves. Most people do not have as much time as they would like to go around in them. Besides those few people who have enough money to buy what they want, most people cannot purchase everything they desire and there are many who cannot afford to buy even what they need. As long as they can pay the price they can select what they want from the abundance. But if they cannot afford it, they must be content only with browsing in these places. However, the Messenger of Allah ﷺ tells us that people can have as much as they want of everything in the markets of the Garden. There, it will not be a matter of shopping; everyone will be able to have whatever he likes. There will be a variety of blessings in these markets that people have never seen or even imagined before. In His great kindness, Allah will give everyone what they desire and no one will want for anything.

This situation is described in the hadith:

So we will come to a market surrounded by angels in which there is that which eyes have never seen the like of, the ears have never heard and which has never occurred to human hearts. That which we desire will be carried to us, and nothing will be sold in it or bought. In that market the people of the Garden will meet each other, so that a man of high rank will come forward and meet those who are lesser than h i m s e l f [and none of them will be low people] and the clothes he has on will amaze and delight him. Be-fore he ceases speaking, an even finer raiment will appear upon him. That is because it is not fitting for anyone to sorrow in it. (Narrated by Abu Hurayra, Sunan Ibn Majah; at-Tirmidhi)

There is in the Garden a market wherein there will be no buying and selling, but forms of men and women. So when a man wishes a form, he will enter into it. (Narrated by Ali, at-Tirmidhi)

Another blessing mentioned in the hadith is the physical features of men and women. To be able to change one's style at will and to appear wearing different fashions is something that many people in this world dream about. Most people would like to have a beautiful, healthy and un-blemished face and body. From birth, people have been given a certain hair colour, iris colour, facial features, skin tone, and height and body type. However, in the Garden there is no worldly sense of monotony from the existence of one kind of beauty; a person's looks change when and however he may desire, as in this hadith containing the transformation of the man's clothing in an instant. This is another blessing.

In another hadith, we are told about the pleasant social life in the markets of the Garden where believers sit in beautiful, fragrant, comfort-able places, and meet and converse with one another:

It is certain that there are such markets in the Garden in which no goods are exchanged. When the inmates of the Garden arrive there, they will recline on fresh and bright pearly earth of musk. They will meet with each other as they did in this world. They will talk of how they were in this world and how they worshipped our Lord, of how they enlivened the nights in prayer, of how they fasted during the day, of the wealth and poverty of the world, of death… and of how they are the people of the Garden. (Mukhtasar Tadhkirah al-Qurtubi, p. 326/565)

The Food of the Garden

In both the Qur'an and the hadith we are told that there are many delicious foods in the Garden. In particular meat and various fruits will be offered in abundance to the inmates of the Garden. Allah tells us in the Qur'an about the quality of these gifts to the People of the Garden:

And any fruit they specify and any bird-meat they desire... (Surat al-Waqi'a: 20-21)

... as recompense for what they did. (Surat al-Waqi'a: 24)

We are also told that some of the blessings offered to the People of the Garden resemble things in this world. In one verse, Allah says:

Give the good news to those who have iman and do right actions that they will have Gardens with rivers flowing under them. When they are given fruit there as provision, they will say, "This is what we were given before." But they were only given a simulation of it.

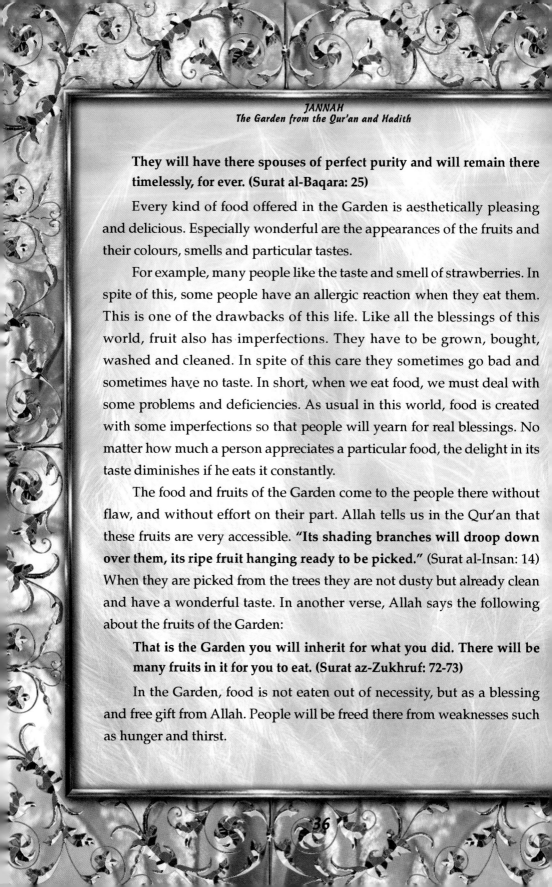

They will have there spouses of perfect purity and will remain there timelessly, for ever. (Surat al-Baqara: 25)

Every kind of food offered in the Garden is aesthetically pleasing and delicious. Especially wonderful are the appearances of the fruits and their colours, smells and particular tastes.

For example, many people like the taste and smell of strawberries. In spite of this, some people have an allergic reaction when they eat them. This is one of the drawbacks of this life. Like all the blessings of this world, fruit also has imperfections. They have to be grown, bought, washed and cleaned. In spite of this care they sometimes go bad and sometimes have no taste. In short, when we eat food, we must deal with some problems and deficiencies. As usual in this world, food is created with some imperfections so that people will yearn for real blessings. No matter how much a person appreciates a particular food, the delight in its taste diminishes if he eats it constantly.

The food and fruits of the Garden come to the people there without flaw, and without effort on their part. Allah tells us in the Qur'an that these fruits are very accessible. **"Its shading branches will droop down over them, its ripe fruit hanging ready to be picked."** (Surat al-Insan: 14) When they are picked from the trees they are not dusty but already clean and have a wonderful taste. In another verse, Allah says the following about the fruits of the Garden:

That is the Garden you will inherit for what you did. There will be many fruits in it for you to eat. (Surat az-Zukhruf: 72-73)

In the Garden, food is not eaten out of necessity, but as a blessing and free gift from Allah. People will be freed there from weaknesses such as hunger and thirst.

The people with taqwa will be
amid shade and fountains and
have any fruits that they desire:
"Eat and drink with relish
for what you did."
(Surat al-Mursalat: 41-43)

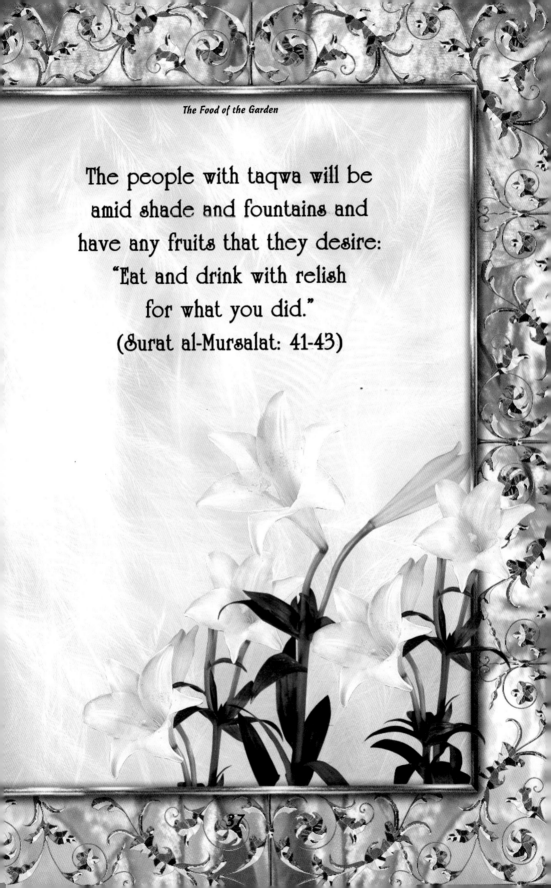

A quality of the blessings of the Garden mentioned in both the Qur'an and the hadith is their abundance. Allah revealed in Surah Sad that provision there will be without cost and will never be used up:

This is what you are promised on the Day of Reckoning. This is Our provision which will never run out. (Surah Sad: 53-54)

The Abundance of Fruit:

In this world, fruits are pure foods that clean the body of toxins and give resistance to disease; they are very rich in vitamins and minerals, and are refreshing and give health and even beauty. The Messenger of Allah ﷺ said the following about this blessing of the Garden:

When opened, each fruit of the lote-tree of the Garden yields seventy-two colours and types of food, and no colour or type is like any other. (Mukhtasar Tadhkirah al-Qurtubi, p. 312/517)

The Messenger ﷺ drew attention to the colour and variety of fruit in the Garden. The fact that they are so different from one another will be pleasing to people. They will not always have the same shape, smell, taste or colour; they will be created in such a variety that people will be surprised and excited because every time they see them will be like the very first time. These are only one of the manifestations of Allah's endless creative power and artistry. This variety, which in the world is already overwhelming, will be without limit in the Garden.

The blessings of the Garden will be presented to its people in the most pleasant way. Allah will give them a banquet and servants created for this service will serve the various fruits to them on gold and silver trays, doing so with pleasure and attention. In one verse, Allah says:

We are your protectors in the life of this world and the Hereafter. You

will have there all that your selves could wish for. You will have there everything you demand. Hospitality from One Who is Ever-Forgiving, Most Merciful. (Surah Fussilat: 31-32)

A Bedouin came to the Prophet ﷺ and asked him "Is there fruit there?" He said, "Yes, and there is a tree called Tuba," and he mentioned something which I do not know what it was. The Bedouin asked, "What tree of this land does it resemble?" He said, "It does not resemble any tree of your land. Have you been to Syria?" He said, "No." He said, "It resembles a tree in Syria called al-Jawzah (walnut) which grows with one trunk then spreads out its branches higher up." The Bedouin asked, "How big is its trunk?" He said, "If one of the camels of your people was to go around it, it would not complete one circuit before its neck broke of old age and exhaustion." The Bedouin asked, "Are there grapes there?" He said, "Yes." He asked, "How big is a bunch?" He said, "The distance a crow could fly without stopping in a month." He asked, "How big is one grape?" He said, "Does your father ever slaughter a he-goat from his flocks?" He said, "Yes." He said, "And does he skin it and give the hide to your mother, and say, 'Make me a bucket'?" He said, "Yes." The Bedouin asked, "Is one grape big enough to satisfy me and my family?" He said, "Yes, and your whole tribe." (Reported by 'Utbah ibn 'Abdin al-Salami, Ahmad ibn Hanbal)

When we consider the fruits of the Garden, we must not think in terms of this world's limitations. In the above hadith, the Prophet ﷺ gave examples of only a few fruits, but the Garden is a place where everything desired will be provided in a most wonderful way; there are many other blessings there that do not occur to our minds but will give us great pleasure.

Here are some verses from the Qur'an in which Allah mentions the fruits of the Garden:

Amid thornless lote-trees and banana-trees [with fruits]. (Surat al-Waqi'a: 28-29)

In them are fruits and date-palms and pomegranates. (Surat ar-Rahman: 68)

And fruits in abundance never failing, unrestricted. (Surat al-Waqi'a: 32-33)

They will have preordained provision: sweet fruits and high honour in Gardens of Delight. (Surat as-Saffat: 41-43)

Examples of the Food in the Garden:
Dates:

There is a story about dates in the hadith:

Someone asked, "O Prophet! Are there dates in the Garden? Because I love dates." And the Prophet ﷺ replied: "Yes, there are dates… the dates of the Garden have golden branches. They have golden shoots. They have leaves as beautiful as the finest clothing anyone has ever seen. There are golden bunches of dates. Even the stalks of these bunches of dates are of gold. At the base of each golden date are sticky scales. They have fruits like giant jars, softer than foam, sweeter than honey." (Mukhtasar Tadhkirah al-Qurtubi, p. 315/522)

We notice here that every detail of the Garden is compared with the most attractive things that we know and understand, and the descriptions of their appearances and delicious taste show what blessings they are. For example, beneath the branches of the date trees in the Garden, the leaves look like beautiful silk fabric.

Another hadith tells about the size of the dates:

The branches of the date trees in the Garden are green emerald. Their shoots are reddish gold. Their leaves are clothing to be worn by the Peo-

ple of the Garden. One part are undergarments, one part are lined over-
garments. The fruits of the date of the Garden are like great jars and jugs.
There are no seeds within them. (Mukhtasar Tadhkirah al-Qurtubi, p.
314)

In the above hadith the dates are likened to jewels and it is said that,
by Allah's will, their appearance and their taste will be perfect.

Figs:

According to one hadith, our Prophet ﷺ said the following about
figs:

If I had to mention a fruit that descended from the Garden I would say
this is it… (Mukhtasar Tadhkirah al-Qurtubi, p. 313)

Figs are also mentioned in the Qur'an (Surat at-Tin: 1). Figs have one
of the highest mineral contents of all fruits and have a special place as a
food that is high in energy.

Watermelons:

In one of his hadith, our Prophet ﷺ says the following about mel-
ons:

Benefit from the watermelon and respect it, because its juice is from the
Garden and its taste is from the Garden … the watermelon is [one of the
fruits] of the Garden. (Mukhtasar Tadhkirah al-Qurtubi, p. 313)

Bananas:

In a verse in which the Garden is described, Allah speaks of bananas
in this way:

Amid thornless lote-trees and banana-trees [with fruits], one above another and extended shade and water flowing constantly and abundant fruit, neither intercepted nor forbidden. **(Surat al-Waqi'a: 28-33)**

With their aroma, delicious taste and numerous benefits, bananas are a favourite fruit of many people. But, as with all other blessings, the bananas in the Garden are much more wonderful, delicious and aromatic than in this world.

Meat:

Besides fruit, meat is also mentioned in the Qur'an and the hadith. In one verse of the Qur'an, Allah tells us that meat is a blessing of the Garden:

We will supply them with any kind of fruit and meat that they desire. (Surat at-Tur: 22)

The Messenger 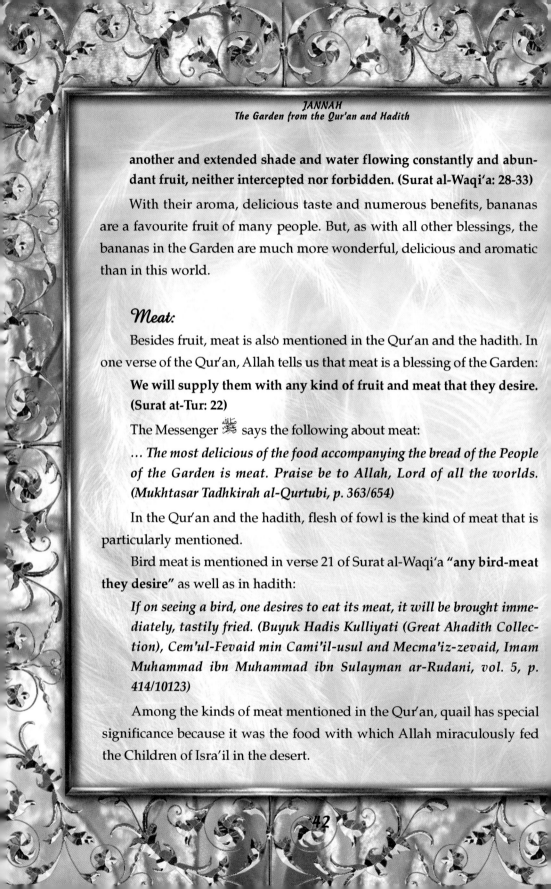 says the following about meat:

… The most delicious of the food accompanying the bread of the People of the Garden is meat. Praise be to Allah, Lord of all the worlds. (Mukhtasar Tadhkirah al-Qurtubi, p. 363/654)

In the Qur'an and the hadith, flesh of fowl is the kind of meat that is particularly mentioned.

Bird meat is mentioned in verse 21 of Surat al-Waqi'a **"any bird-meat they desire"** as well as in hadith:

If on seeing a bird, one desires to eat its meat, it will be brought immediately, tastily fried. (Buyuk Hadis Kulliyati (Great Ahadith Collection), Cem'ul-Fevaid min Cami'il-usul and Mecma'iz-zevaid, Imam Muhammad ibn Muhammad ibn Sulayman ar-Rudani, vol. 5, p. 414/10123)

Among the kinds of meat mentioned in the Qur'an, quail has special significance because it was the food with which Allah miraculously fed the Children of Isra'il in the desert.

Human Beauty in the Garden

One of the greatest delights in this world is human beauty. If a person lives in a wonderful house, eats the finest food and goes on holiday to the most wonderful places, the pleasure he takes from these things will be limited if he is alone. All these only have meaning if they are shared with others. Allah has breathed spirit into the human being and he is of value because of his worship of Allah, obedience and character. If perfect physical beauty accompanies these qualities, the blessing becomes complete, and is something that everyone can appreciate.

Here is a hadith in which human beauty in the Garden is described:

The maidens of the Garden are like ruby and coral. One looks at one maiden's face and sees himself even more clearly than he would in a mirror, and the smallest jewel therein will illuminate the east and the west. *(Ahmad Diya ad-Din al-Kamushkhanawi, Ramuz al-Ahadith, vol. 2, p. 337/7)*

The Messenger of Allah 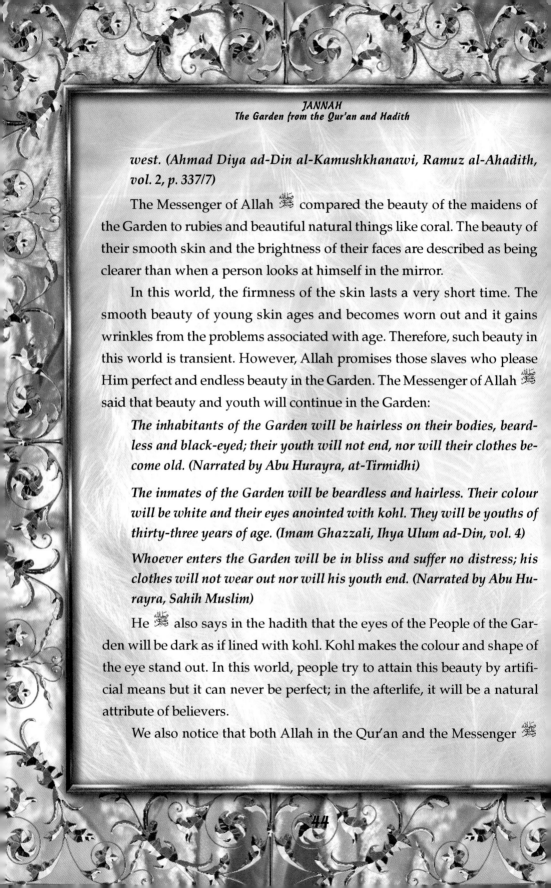 compared the beauty of the maidens of the Garden to rubies and beautiful natural things like coral. The beauty of their smooth skin and the brightness of their faces are described as being clearer than when a person looks at himself in the mirror.

In this world, the firmness of the skin lasts a very short time. The smooth beauty of young skin ages and becomes worn out and it gains wrinkles from the problems associated with age. Therefore, such beauty in this world is transient. However, Allah promises those slaves who please Him perfect and endless beauty in the Garden. The Messenger of Allah said that beauty and youth will continue in the Garden:

The inhabitants of the Garden will be hairless on their bodies, beardless and black-eyed; their youth will not end, nor will their clothes become old. (Narrated by Abu Hurayra, at-Tirmidhi)

The inmates of the Garden will be beardless and hairless. Their colour will be white and their eyes anointed with kohl. They will be youths of thirty-three years of age. (Imam Ghazzali, Ihya Ulum ad-Din, vol. 4)

Whoever enters the Garden will be in bliss and suffer no distress; his clothes will not wear out nor will his youth end. (Narrated by Abu Hurayra, Sahih Muslim)

He also says in the hadith that the eyes of the People of the Garden will be dark as if lined with kohl. Kohl makes the colour and shape of the eye stand out. In this world, people try to attain this beauty by artificial means but it can never be perfect; in the afterlife, it will be a natural attribute of believers.

We also notice that both Allah in the Qur'an and the Messenger in his hadith speak about the sweet nature of women in the Garden. In another verse of the Qur'an Allah tells us of the people in the Garden and the beauty of their environment and of the maidens there:

In them are sweet, lovely maidens. (Surat ar-Rahman: 70)

In another hadith, the beauty of the people in the Garden is described thus:

… Each maiden has seventy sets of clothing, all of different colours. Likewise, each is given seventy different scents… Each maiden has seventy thousand female servants and seventy thousand male servants to serve and attend to her needs. Each servant is accompanied by golden trays with different foods, in which believers will find new flavours not found in the one before… (Mukhtasar Tadhkirah al-Qurtubi, p. 333/591)

In many hadith the Prophet 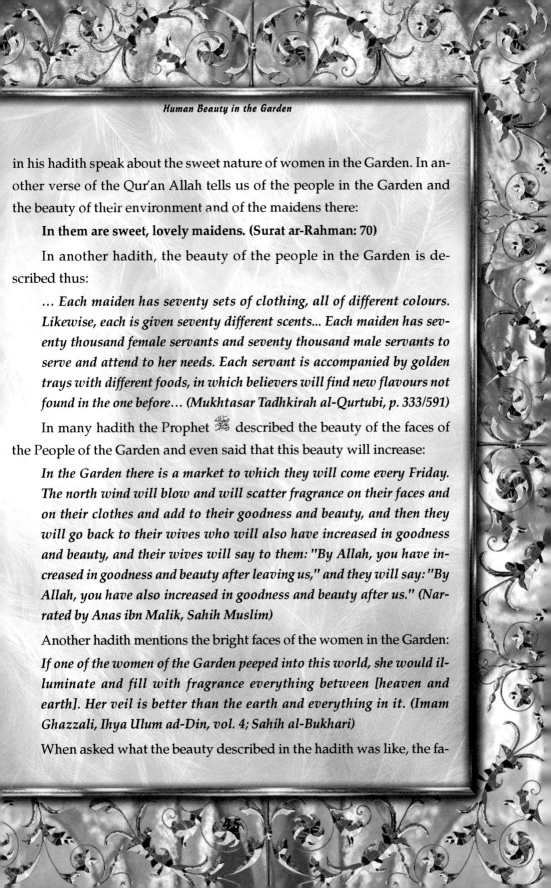 described the beauty of the faces of the People of the Garden and even said that this beauty will increase:

In the Garden there is a market to which they will come every Friday. The north wind will blow and will scatter fragrance on their faces and on their clothes and add to their goodness and beauty, and then they will go back to their wives who will also have increased in goodness and beauty, and their wives will say to them: "By Allah, you have increased in goodness and beauty after leaving us," and they will say: "By Allah, you have also increased in goodness and beauty after us." (Narrated by Anas ibn Malik, Sahih Muslim)

Another hadith mentions the bright faces of the women in the Garden:

If one of the women of the Garden peeped into this world, she would illuminate and fill with fragrance everything between [heaven and earth]. Her veil is better than the earth and everything in it. (Imam Ghazzali, Ihya Ulum ad-Din, vol. 4; Sahih al-Bukhari)

When asked what the beauty described in the hadith was like, the famous scholar, Bediuzzaman, answered:

> *Its meaning is truly beautiful and its beauty is most lovely. It is like this: in this world, which is ugly, inanimate, lifeless, and for the most part just a husk, beauty and loveliness only appear beautiful to the eye, and so long as familiarity is not an obstacle, that is sufficient. Whereas in the Garden, which is beautiful, living, brilliant, and entirely essence without husk and kernel without shell, like the eye, all man's senses and subtle faculties will want to receive their different pleasures and various delights from the houris [maidens of the Garden],… and from the women of this world, who will be like houris and even more beautiful… That is to say, just as the houris are clothed in seventy of the varieties of the adornments of the Garden, and not just one sort, none of which conceal the others; so they display beauty and loveliness perhaps seventy times greater than their own bodies and beings, all of different sorts and varieties. (Bediuzzaman Said Nursi, Risale-i Nur Collection, The Words, The Twenty-Eighth Word)*

The Beauty and Variety of Clothing in the Garden:

Everyone likes to wear fine clothing of quality fabrics, and the various colours of the beautiful clothing of the Garden will appeal to all the people there. No matter how fine clothing is in this world, there will always be some imperfection. In time, all clothing becomes old, its colours fade and the wearer loses the pleasure he had when he first wore it. How much clothing a person has in this world is not important, because the pleasure he derives from it is limited by his lifespan, among other things. Like all other things, this too is left behind at the time of death. However, clothing in the Garden is flawless in its beauty and variety and lasts forever.

The clothing of the people of the Garden is created for their comfort. The clothing they wear will not cause them any discomfort in the perfect beauty of the Garden. In the Garden, clothing does not fade, wrinkle, become soiled or grow old as it does in this world, and there are no preparatory stages such as weaving the fabric and sewing the garment. By Allah's blessing, everything in the Garden is already perfectly prepared. Here are some more details about the clothing believers will wear in the Garden:

... The garments of the Garden are not woven. The fruits of the Garden split open and garments emerge from them... (Mukhtasar Tadhkirah al-Qurtubi, p. 21)

Whoever enters the Garden will live in happiness. He will want for nothing, his clothing will not grow old and his youth will not end. (Imam Ghazzali, Ihya Ulum ad-Din, vol. 4)

...the leaves [of the date-palms in the Garden] are clothing to be worn by the people of the Garden. One part are undergarments, one part are lined over-garment. (Mukhtasar Tadhkirah al-Qurtubi, p. 314)

... They [the inmates of the Garden] will proclaim the glory of Allah morning and evening... each wife will have seventy dresses. (Imam Ghazzali, Ihya Ulum ad-Din, vol. 4)

Allah also says in the Qur'an that clothing will be rich and made of silk:

They will wear green garments of fine silk and rich brocade... (Surat al-Insan: 21)

But Allah will admit those who have iman and do right actions into Gardens with rivers flowing under them where they will be adorned with gold bracelets and pearls, and where their clothing will be of silk. (Surat al-Hajj: 23)

The Natural Beauty of the Garden

The human spirit has been created so that it takes pleasure in form, symmetry, beauty, purity, order, harmony of colour, in short, in perfection. All colours and sights in nature correspond most to this delight in the human spirit.

The places that people choose to relax and be comfortable in are often closely associated with natural beauty: woods, forests, seacoasts and river banks. With their clean air and open spaces and often near water, these give people a sense of well-being and happiness.

Places far from natural beauty where there is no sunshine and fresh air do not appeal to human beings.

One of the reasons why we human beings look for natural beauty is because Allah has created us to take pleasure in the beauties of the Garden. Whether a person is aware of it or not, he is waiting for the blessings of the Garden. Allah describes the Garden to us in the Qur'an with all the attributes of nature:

But those who have iman and do right actions will have Gardens

with rivers flowing under them. That is the Great Victory. (Surat al-Buruj: 11)

Shaded by spreading branches. (Surat ar-Rahman: 48)

The Trees of the Garden:

We enjoy being in places where trees grow. If we live in the middle of crowded cities, we generally would like to be in places where there are trees and green spaces. We take pleasure in the sight of an area with trees and we even like looking at photographs or paintings of such places. Trees have been created to be of great benefit for the earth and they are a blessing offered to us by our Lord. With their wonderful appearances, type and colour variations, and the pleasing shade they provide, trees have been created for human pleasure. The Prophet ﷺ mentioned the enormous dimensions of the trees of the Garden, illustrating it by mention of their shade:

In the Garden, there is a tree under whose shade a rider could travel for a hundred years without covering [the distance] completely. (Narrated by Sahl ibn Sa'd, Sahih Muslim)

In the Garden there is a tree under whose shade a rider can travel for one-hundred years. And if you wish, you can recite: "and wide-spreading shade." (Qur'an 56:30) (Narrated by Abu Hurayra, Sahih al-Bukhari)

In the Qur'an Allah describes shade as a blessing:

But as for those who have iman and do right actions, We will admit them into Gardens with rivers flowing under them, remaining in them timelessly, for ever and ever. In them they will have spouses of perfect purity and We will admit them into cool, refreshing shade. (Surat an-Nisa': 57)

What is the Garden promised to those who have taqwa like? It has rivers flowing under it and its foodstuffs and cool shade never fail. That is the final fate of those who have taqwa. But the final fate of the kuffar is the Fire. (Surat ar-Ra'd: 35)

They and their wives reclining on couches in the shade. (Surah Ya Sin: 56)

The people with taqwa will be amid shade and fountains. (Surat al-Mursalat: 41)

Reclining in it on couches, they will experience there neither burning sun nor bitter cold. (Surat al-Insan: 13)

In several hadith, our Prophet ﷺ describes the trees of the Garden:

The trunk of every tree in the Garden is of gold. (At-Tirmidhi)

In the Garden we will witness Allah's incomparable and endless creation in which everything is possible. For example, the fruit of the trees in the Garden will resemble rubies, diamonds, sapphires and other precious stones but become edible when people pick them.

The Rivers and Seas in the Garden:

Sources of water are abundant, refreshing and cleansing, and places near water often have a climate that is both more liveable and pleasing to people because of its temperateness. For this reason, places that people choose for relaxation are often near the sea, on lake-shores or on the banks of rivers. So, in the Qur'an, Allah, glorious is He and exalted, says that those who have taqwa will, by Allah's mercy, be **"amid Gardens and Springs."** (Surat al-Hijr: 45)

The Prophet 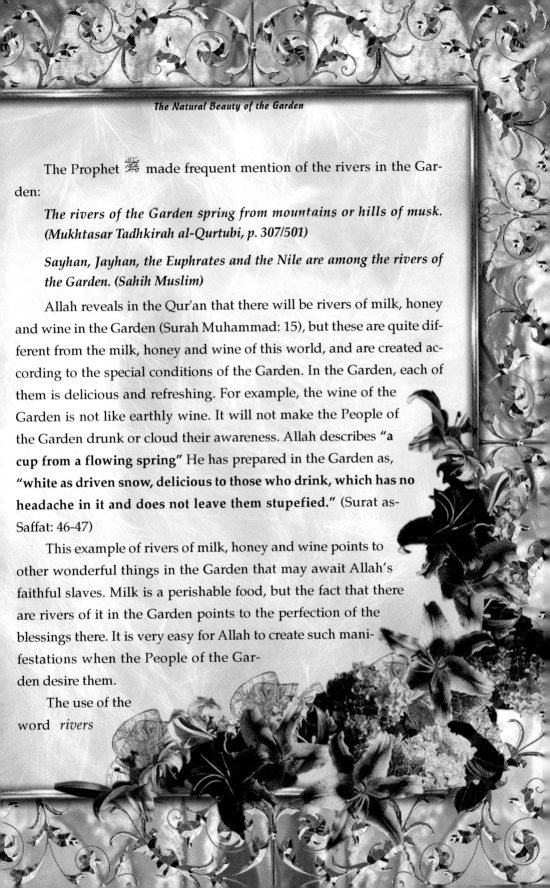 made frequent mention of the rivers in the Garden:

The rivers of the Garden spring from mountains or hills of musk.
(Mukhtasar Tadhkirah al-Qurtubi, p. 307/501)

Sayhan, Jayhan, the Euphrates and the Nile are among the rivers of
the Garden. (Sahih Muslim)

Allah reveals in the Qur'an that there will be rivers of milk, honey and wine in the Garden (Surah Muhammad: 15), but these are quite different from the milk, honey and wine of this world, and are created according to the special conditions of the Garden. In the Garden, each of them is delicious and refreshing. For example, the wine of the Garden is not like earthly wine. It will not make the People of the Garden drunk or cloud their awareness. Allah describes **"a cup from a flowing spring"** He has prepared in the Garden as, **"white as driven snow, delicious to those who drink, which has no headache in it and does not leave them stupefied."** (Surat as-Saffat: 46-47)

This example of rivers of milk, honey and wine points to other wonderful things in the Garden that may await Allah's faithful slaves. Milk is a perishable food, but the fact that there are rivers of it in the Garden points to the perfection of the blessings there. It is very easy for Allah to create such manifestations when the People of the Garden desire them.

The use of the word *rivers*

emphasises the abundance of these blessings in the Garden. In this world, people can only have a limited number of these blessings, in jars, glass bottles and in other types of packaging, but the fact that there are never-ending and unadulterated streams of them in the Garden is a wondrous blessing.

These rivers are described in detail in the Qur'an:

An image of the Garden which is promised to those who have taqwa: in it there are rivers of water which will never spoil and rivers of milk whose taste will never change and rivers of wine, delightful to all who drink it, and rivers of honey of undiluted purity; in it they will have fruit of every kind and forgiveness from their Lord... (Surah Muhammad: 15)

In this verse Allah gives examples including water, milk, honey and wine. But it is possible for rivers of other imperishable blessings, abundant and pure as water, to flow for the delight of the believers. Allah tells us that drinks will be offered in goblets in the Garden, and that the People of the Garden will not get headaches from them or lose their self-composure. In another verse of the Qur'an, Allah says, **"a cup from a flowing spring passing round among them."** (Surat as-Saffat: 45) The inmates of the Garden, **"... are given the choicest sealed wine to drink, whose seal is musk – mixed with Tasnim,"** which has been prepared for believers (Surat al-Mutaffifin: 25-27). Tasnim is a fountain in the Garden.

Allah, exalted is He, also says in the Qur'an that these beverages are fragrant.

The Beautiful Landscape of the Garden:

The Prophet ﷺ described the beauty of the landscape of the Garden:

[It is built of] one brick of gold and one brick of silver, its mortar is of strongly scented musk, its stones are pearls and emeralds, and its soil is of saffron ... (At-Tirmidhi; Ahmad ibn Hanbal, Musnad)

In this hadith, the soil of the Garden is said to be saffron, a spice and dyestuff obtained from a valuable plant. This plant, with its vanilla-like aroma and its bright golden colour is a very special spice. To obtain one kilogram of saffron, between 70 thousand and 250 thousand flowers must be picked. Today, the production of saffron decreases daily. The most important factor in this is the difficulty in growing the plant because it takes between 3-4 years for saffron to be harvested. That such a valuable plant, which is grown with such difficulty in this world, is so plentiful in the Garden that it covers the whole landscape shows that the blessings there will be beyond reckoning.

The Expanse of the Garden:

When the People of the Garden settle in Allah's Garden a wide space will be left over. There, Allah will populate three hundred and sixty worlds, each one of which is larger than the world from its creation to its end. (Ahmad Diya ad-Din al-Kamushkhanawi, Ramuz al-Aha-dith, vol. 1, p. 30/5)

As the Prophet ﷺ points out in this hadith, there is vast spaciousness in the Garden. Contrary to the narrow restriction of the Fire described in the Qur'an, the Garden is expansive. It has been created in this way so that the human spirit may delight in open horizons and take pleasure in its expanse. Allah, in the Qur'an, describes the breadth of the Garden in these words:

Race each other to forgiveness from your Lord and a Garden as wide as the heavens and the earth, prepared for the people who have taqwa. (Surah Al 'Imran: 133)

The Fragrant Aromas of the Garden

Fragrant aromas are a gift that Allah has given us. In this world, the most beautiful scent only lasts a short time. The molecules of a particular scent evaporate into the air and our noses quickly become used to the scent; this limits the pleasure that we can obtain from a scent. But the duration of a scent can be as important as the immediate pleasure it gives. In his hadith the Prophet ﷺ describes the delight that beautiful aromas from the Garden can give:

If one of the women of the Garden peeped into this world, she would illuminate and fill with fragrance everything between [heaven and earth]. (Sahih al-Bukhari; Imam Ghazzali, Ihya Ulum ad-Din, vol. 4)

In another hadith, the Messenger of Allah ﷺ told us about the beautiful aromas of the food in the Garden:

… the best smelling and finest foods are produced. (Al-Hafiz ibn ad-Dayba ash-Shaybani, Taysir al-usul ila Jami al-usul, p. 448/3)

Aroma is an important element in the pleasure we derive from food. The pleasure we take from the scent of a cake in the oven comes from the aroma of the vanilla and the chocolate, for example, wafting through the

...whereas those who have iman
and do right actions will be in
the lush Meadows of the Gardens.
They will have whatever they
wish for with their Lord. That
is the great favour.
(Surat ash-Shura: 22)

air. In the same way, the pleasure we take from roasting meat, oranges, tomatoes or any other food is due to the aromas they exude. If we had no sense of smell we would not be able to distinguish the foods we eat in this particular fashion and we would not experience their tastes in quite the same way. From this point of view, smells are complementary to the pleasure we find in delicious tastes.

Another hadith mentions the beauty of the aromas of the Garden:

The north wind will blow and will scatter fragrance on their faces and on their clothes and add to their goodness and beauty. (Narrated by Anas, Sahih Muslim)

Another hadith speaks of plants that are known by their beautiful scents:

Henna [a dye and scent] is the chief scent of the Garden... When Allah created the Garden He filled it with the scent of sweet basil, and surrounded the sweet basil with the scent of henna... (Mukhtasar Tadhkirah al-Qurtubi, p. 342/619)

Basil, mentioned in the hadith, is one of the plants known for its beautiful scent. However, the scents we know in this world are only a pale reflection of those in the Garden, and Allah knows best.

All aromas in the Garden have been created as blessings to please the senses of the believers, and none of the unpleasant odours we often encounter in this world will be found there. Those foul odours remind people of the imperfections of this world and make them long for the Garden. There will be no such imperfections in the Garden and every place will be redolent of the sweet aromas that please the human spirit. In one of his hadith, the Prophet ﷺ says the following of the Garden:

... its mortar is of strongly scented musk ... (At-Tirmidhi)

The Beautiful Voices and Conversations of the Garden

Among the reasons why those who live in this world without the teachings of the Qur'an are sad and anxious is because they always have to deal with conversations that are filled with apprehension, pessimism, dishonesty and negativity. Even the slightest negativity in conversations can make the best environment uncomfortable. On the other hand, a heartfelt compliment, a word spoken to honour someone, a word that evokes pleasure, courage and hope, or an honest and sincere conversation are sometimes more important than the material blessings surrounding us. In this world, we often encounter conversations that make us uncomfortable. However, Allah tells us that there will be no such things in the Garden; believers will have delightful conversations with one another in comfortable surroundings. Along with the great blessings of sincere converse that Allah's beloved slaves will have in the Garden, believers will also be far removed from lies and empty, negative chatter. In the Qur'an, Allah tells us that this will be a wonderful gift for His slaves:

Where they will hear no prattle and no denial, a recompense from your Lord, a commensurate gift. (Surat an-Naba': 35-36)

The Messenger ﷺ also tells us about the beauty of the conversations in the Garden:

Allah will fill the ears of the person of the Garden with people's praise of him, which he will hear. Allah will fill the ears of the person of the Fire with people's evil remembrance of him, which he will hear. (Ahmad Diya ad-Din al-Kamushkhanawi, Ramuz al-Ahadith, vol. 1, p. 155/2)

Some hadith also indicate that the sincere converse that believers

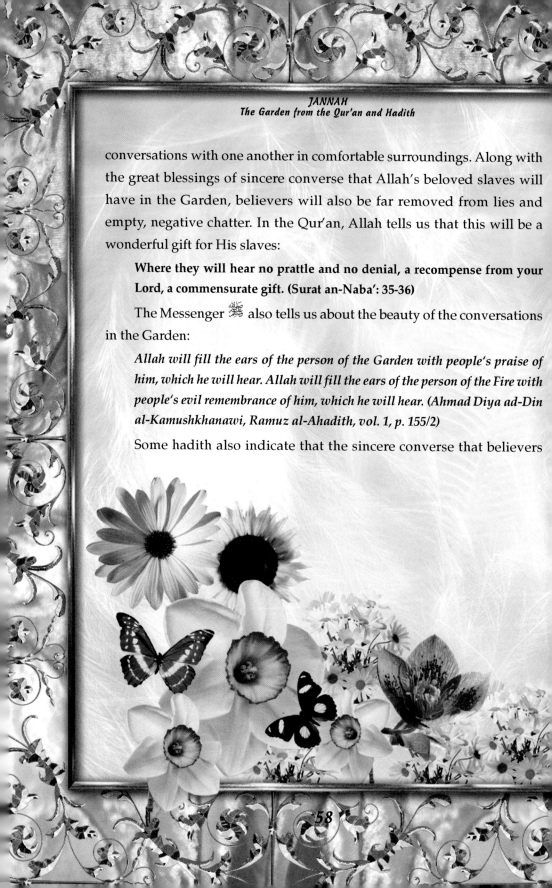

have in this world will continue in the afterlife. Another hadith tells us that, in their conversations in the Garden, believers will recall what they have done in their earthly lives:

> *When the people of the Garden settle in the Garden some brothers will wish to see each other. One will go to one side of a couch and the other to the other. When they meet they will remember and speak together of the things between them in this world. One will say, "My brother, do you remember how we prayed to Allah in such and such a mosque in the world? And Allah has forgiven us." (Ahmad Diya ad-Din al-Kamushkhanawi, Ramuz al-Ahadith, vol. 1, p. 29/12)*

Beautiful Sounds in the Garden:

Beautiful sounds are another blessing given to believers in the Garden. In the world, shrill noises, music with static in the background, noisy surroundings, loud motors and sirens make our environment uncomfortable even if they only last a short time. So screaming, shouting and cries of anguish or pain make believers think about the Fire. As the Prophet ﷺ told us, in the Garden everyone's voice will be beautiful and every sound that strikes the ear will be pleasant. The beautiful sounds of the Garden are described in the following hadith:

> *There will certainly be an assembly of the dark-eyed maidens who will raise up voices the like of which people will not have heard. (Narrated by Ali, at-Tirmidhi)*

Eternal Life and Youth in the Garden

In this world human life may last 6-7 decades on average, which is a very short time. Allah tells us in the Qur'an the kinds of things people will say about their earthly lives on the Last Day:

He will say, "How many years did you tarry on the earth?" They will say, "We tarried there for a day or part of a day. Ask those able to count!" (Surat al-Muminun: 112-113)

However, in the Garden life is limitless. Allah tells us in the Qur'an that the believers will be immortal and that their blessings will be eternal; "They will not taste any death there – except for the first one..." (Surat ad-Dukhan: 56). We must consider carefully the idea of eternity, about which we speak so easily, because it does not refer to a thousand or a million years, but to timelessness. Therefore, people in the Garden will not think about time or calculate it as in this world. Life will not end with the passing of years. Allah revealed this to us in the Qur'an:

> As for those who are glad, they will be in the Garden, remaining in it timelessly, for ever, as long as the heavens and earth endure, except as your Lord wills: an uninterrupted gift. (Surah Hud: 108)

Again in the Qur'an, Allah tells us that the service of ageless youths will be one of the blessings enjoyed in the Garden:

> There will circulate among them, ageless youths. (Surat al-Waqi'a: 17)

The hadith also tell us about the endless life of the Garden:

Allah will admit the inmates of the Garden into the Garden and the inmates of the Fire into the Fire. Then the announcer will stand between them and say: "O inmates of the Garden, there is no death for you, O inmates of the Fire, there is no death for you. You will live forever therein." (Sahih Muslim, vol. 4)

Whoever enters the Garden will be in bliss and suffer no distress; his clothes will not wear out nor will his youth end. (Ahmad, Musnad; at-Tirmidhi; Narrated by Abu Hurayra, Sahih Muslim)

No matter how beautiful, wealthy or healthy a person is, he cannot escape death. Therefore, even if a person is wealthier than others, the conditions of this world determine that this wealth can come to an end and he may even be left destitute. One reason why worldly blessings are transitory is because we desire the real and original blessings of the Garden. All the beautiful things we see and the pleasures we enjoy in this world are imperfect and transitory. However, these blessings in the Garden have been created without being subject to time or causality. For this reason the blessings of the Garden will last forever. In the Qur'an, Allah announces the glad tidings of this eternity that will be enjoyed in the Garden:

Their Lord gives them the good news of His mercy and good pleasure and Gardens where they will enjoy everlasting delight, remaining in them timelessly, for ever and ever. Truly there is an immense reward with Allah. (Surat at-Tawba: 21-22)

[Those who have iman will be] remaining in them timelessly, for ever, with no desire to move away from them. (Surat al-Kahf: 108)

Eternal Youth in the Garden:

Those who are remote from the teachings of the Qur'an are even afraid of growing old while young. They think about the sickness and helplessness that old age brings and are worried about whether or not there will be someone to look after them when they get to that point. There are many people who have such anxieties, who look pessimistically towards old age.

Beginning in our 20's cell renewal in our bodies slows down and our skin starts to lose its former elasticity. With the passing years the effects of ageing become visible. This worries people. They sorrow as they watch their youth slip away. Of course, this scenario applies to people who have no iman. Believers submit to Allah in all the illnesses and weaknesses they may encounter in this transitory world; as an act of worship they accept every-thing that happens to them and, unlike those who have no *deen*, they live their lives without regret or fear and anxiety. Moreover, they realise that the good things of this world are intrinsically flawed and that the real life is the timeless life of the world to come. And they make every effort hoping to attain the Garden.

Life in this world is fleeting and temporary. Allah has already created all the real blessings of the Garden, just as He has already created the torments of the Fire. On the Last Day He will grant the blessings to His faithful slaves. People in the Garden will always be young, attractive, healthy and robust.

No matter how long an individual may live within the limitations of this life, no matter how late the signs of ageing appear, and no matter how healthy he is, his life will certainly come to an end one day. However, Allah points out in the Qur'an as does the Prophet ﷺ that eternal youth will be one of the blessings of the Garden:

The people of the Garden will enter the Garden hairless on their bodies, beardless and dark-eyed, aged thirty or thirty-three years old. (Narrated by Mu'adh ibn Jabal, at-Tirmidhi)

The thirties are the best time of life when the personality matures and facial features, and the manner of speaking and acting become established. But we must not forget that youthful vigour in the Garden is not the same as it is in this world. That is because under earthly conditions even a young person can live in great helplessness.

Allah has made a new creation in the Hereafter for the inmates of the Garden without any flaw or imperfection. In the Qur'an, Allah tells us about this and in particular how the people of the Garden will be served by eternally young people:

> **Ageless youths will circulate among them, serving them. Seeing them, you would think them scattered pearls. (Surat al-Insan: 19)**

The People of the Garden Are the Same Age:

The fact that the people of the Garden are the same age is a great blessing from Allah. Among people without *deen*, difference in age often leads to discord and lack of communication. People often form groups of persons of the same age in order to feel more relaxed among themselves. Of course, this ought not to apply to Muslims. No matter what age they may be, Muslims should understand one another very well and form friendships with people of any age, older or younger than themselves. The fact that Muslims in the Garden are created the same age as one another is another wonderful blessing from Allah. The Messenger of Allah ﷺ said that the age of the people of the Garden will never change throughout eternity:

> *Whoever of the People of the Garden die, whether while young or old, will be turned into young people of thirty years of age in the Garden, never growing older than that. And thus will be the inmates of the Fire... (Narrated by Abu Sa'id, Sunan Ibn Majah; at-Tirmidhi)*

Another verse of the Qur'an points out that in the Garden the believers' wives will be the same age as them:

> *We have brought maidens into being and made them purest virgins, devoted, passionate, of like age. (Surat al-Waqi'a: 35-37)*

In the Garden All Desires Are Fulfilled

Everything in the universe reflects Allah's infinite power and eternal wisdom. He has created everything in this world as a test and events in it ordinarily occur according to the laws of cause and effect that human reason can grasp. So, when someone sees a fruit, he or she has no doubt that it came from a seed that grew into a tree, bush or plant which in turn yielded the fruit. According to the custom of Allah in His creation, this is the cause of the fruit in this world. However, it must be remembered that, if Allah wished, He could create the whole universe independent of causes. Allah can create what He wants whenever He wants without depending on any logical pattern and without the need for any substance to create from. People should not be deceived by the fact that in this world everything appears to depend on certain causes and natural laws. As the Creator of all causes,

Allah is completely free of them. In the Garden creation will be freed from its need for causes, and so a fruit picked from a tree will immediately be replaced by another, without any loss or decrease. Allah creates both causes and effects. For example, when we look at the shade under a tree, we know it is caused by the angle of the sun's rays. Light and shade are effects of the sun, but Allah makes the sun the cause of light and shade. This is revealed in the Qur'an:

> **Do you not see how your Lord stretches out shadows? If He had wished He could have made them stationary. Then We appoint the sun to be the pointer to them. Then We draw them back to Ourselves in gradual steps. (Surat al-Furqan: 45-46)**

It is as a result of the artistry of Allah that everything in this world is created in a seeming cause-effect relationship. He can create anything in a moment and in the form that He wants, or turn it into any shape He desires. Allah created the universe from nothing, and, at any time He desires He can dissolve the laws – the causes and effects – that we struggle to grasp. In the Garden, faithful Muslims may ask for anything they think will please them and, as soon as they ask for it, they will have it, if Allah wills. Both they themselves and their surroundings will be in the shape and form that they desire; everything they desire will be granted and they will live amid the blessings that will give them the most delight and joy. This will not be in order to supply any need, make up for a deficiency or repair a flaw; it will be a wonderful blessing from Allah simply for the delight of the people of the Garden, and Allah knows best.

Here is an example of this from the hadith:

A man asked the Prophet ﷺ, "Messenger of Allah, are there any horses in the Garden?" He replied: "If Allah makes you enter the Garden, if you wish to ride in it on a horse made of red ruby that will fly you wherever you wish you will do so." At this, another man asked, "Messenger of Allah, are there any camels in the Garden?" but he did not reply as he had to the first man. He said "If Allah makes you enter the Garden you will find everything your self desires and that is pleasing to your eye." (At-Tirmidhi; Al-Hafiz ibn ad-Dayba ash-Shaybani, Taysir al-usul ila Jami al-usul, p. 431/14)

The *everything your self desires and that is pleasing to your eye* mentioned in the hadith is not limited by this world's limitations or our imaginations. In the Qur'an, Allah calls our attention to the richness of His blessings: **"... they will have there all that their hearts desire and their eyes find delight in..."** (Surat az-Zukhruf: 71) Other verses that tell us about this are the following:

... You will have there all that your selves could wish for. You will have there everything you demand. (Surah Fussilat: 31)

... They will remain there timelessly, for ever, among everything their selves desire. (Surat al-Anbiya': 102)

There are many things we desire to do in this world but cannot do, because of lack of time or because there is a risk involved. For example, many people like dangerous sports such as driving fast cars or motorcycles, spending hours deep-sea diving or skiing on high mountain slopes or sky-diving from great heights, but these are all sports that put a person's life at risk.

Others want to play a musical instrument skilfully or wish they had a special talent for painting. Besides talent, such things require expertise and long periods of training. In the Garden, a person can have anything he wants and so he can even have the possibility to do these things whenever he wants without any effort and without the need for any talent, and Allah knows best.

Allah, exalted is He, in the Qur'an, and the Messenger of Allah ﷺ tell us that everything the heart desires is possible if Allah wills. Therefore, a person can enjoy unimaginable things in the next life that are impossible to attain in this world. For example, it is not possible in this world to fly on a horse but we are told in the hadith that this is possible in the Garden. In one hadith the Messenger of Allah ﷺ says that people can fly if they want to:

> *If you are intended for the Garden and say "I would like to ride a horse of red ruby," you will do so. If you say you wish to fly, you will fly. (Ahmad Diya ad-Din al-Kamushkhanawi, Ramuz al-Ahadith, vol. 1, p. 149/5)*

In another hadith, the Prophet ﷺ spoke about the abundance of the blessings in the Garden:

> *The Messenger of Allah ﷺ said that Allah, the Exalted and Glorious, said: "I have prepared for My slaves which no eye has seen, no ear has heard and has never occurred to a human heart …" (Narrated by Abu Hurayra, Sahih Muslim, vol. 4)*

Desires in the Garden Will Be Fulfilled Instantly:

Ordinarily someone who wants to have a fine meal in this world must do some work for it. The most delightful thing would be to have a meal set before us as soon as it came into our minds and not to have to prepare it ourselves. However, such a thing is impossible within the limitations of this world. However, in the Garden, the most pleasing blessings are offered to human beings without their having to make a purchase, or spend time and effort in the process of preparing them. We have an example of this in the hadith:

> *If on seeing a bird, one desires to eat its meat, it will immediately be*

Such people are the Companions
of the Garden, remaining in it
timelessly, for ever, as repayment
for what they did.
(Surat al-Ahqaf: 14)

brought, tastily fried. *(Buyuk Hadis Kulliyati (Great Ahadith Collection),
Cem'ul-Fevaid min Cami'il-usul and Mecma'iz-zevaid, Imam Muhammad
ibn Muhammad ibn Sulayman ar-Rudani, vol. 5, p. 414/10123)*

The following hadith of our Prophet 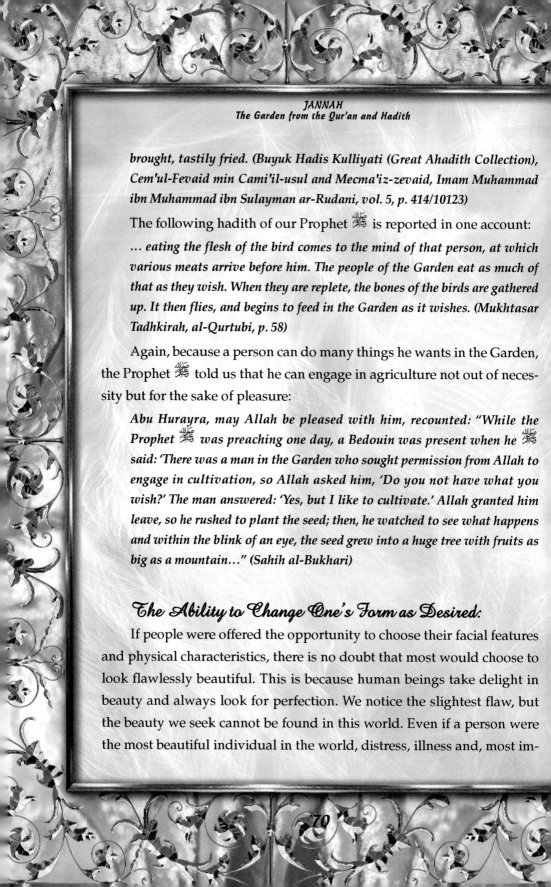 is reported in one account:

*... eating the flesh of the bird comes to the mind of that person, at which
various meats arrive before him. The people of the Garden eat as much of
that as they wish. When they are replete, the bones of the birds are gathered
up. It then flies, and begins to feed in the Garden as it wishes. (Mukhtasar
Tadhkirah, al-Qurtubi, p. 58)*

Again, because a person can do many things he wants in the Garden,
the Prophet ﷺ told us that he can engage in agriculture not out of necessity but for the sake of pleasure:

*Abu Hurayra, may Allah be pleased with him, recounted: "While the
Prophet ﷺ was preaching one day, a Bedouin was present when he ﷺ
said: 'There was a man in the Garden who sought permission from Allah to
engage in cultivation, so Allah asked him, 'Do you not have what you
wish?' The man answered: 'Yes, but I like to cultivate.' Allah granted him
leave, so he rushed to plant the seed; then, he watched to see what happens
and within the blink of an eye, the seed grew into a huge tree with fruits as
big as a mountain..." (Sahih al-Bukhari)*

The Ability to Change One's Form as Desired:

If people were offered the opportunity to choose their facial features
and physical characteristics, there is no doubt that most would choose to
look flawlessly beautiful. This is because human beings take delight in
beauty and always look for perfection. We notice the slightest flaw, but
the beauty we seek cannot be found in this world. Even if a person were
the most beautiful individual in the world, distress, illness and, most im-

portantly, mortality casts a shadow over this beauty. It is a part of our test that every thing in this world has been created with defects and imperfections. There is a good reason for these: to direct us towards the afterlife and make us yearn for the Garden, the real place to find the beauty and perfection that delights us. In the Garden, Allah will recreate people with perfect beauty and give them the most pleasing forms. And this beauty will not be limited to one form. Allah will give His slaves in the Garden the choice of whatever form they desire at any time so that the people of the Garden can have a variety of beautiful forms whenever they want.

The Prophet ﷺ tells us that believers can select a form they like from markets in the Garden and assume it:

> *There is in the Garden a market wherein there will be no buying and selling, but forms of men and women. So when a man wishes a form, he will enter into it. (Narrated by Ali, at-Tirmidhi)*

A Person Who Wants a Child Can Have One:

If people want to have a child, they can have one with the perfect ease characteristic of the Garden:

> *When a believer desires a child in the Garden, its gestation and birth will be in one hour, as he desires. (Sunan Ibn Majah; at-Tirmidhi)*

There Will Be No Night:

In this world, night has been created for rest. There is no need for sleep or rest in the Garden and so there is no need for the darkness of night:

> *There is no night in the Garden. It consists of brightness and light. (Ahmad Diya ad-Din al-Kamushkhanawi, Ramuz al-Ahadith, vol. 2, p. 366/4)*

There Will Be No Sleep:

Sleep is one of the weaknesses that beset us in this world. We have all been created with a need for sleep and cannot resist this urge no matter how much we may want to. Moreover, if the body remains too long without sleep, its resistance to disease is lessened and the individual becomes tired. We spend a great deal of time sleeping: about one third of our lives. Yet, our lives in this world are already short and spending such a large portion of them asleep is like a kind of death. In the Qur'an, Allah says that sleep is similar to death: **"Allah takes back people's selves when their death arrives and those who have not yet died, while they are asleep..."** (Surat az-Zumar: 42) But there is no fatigue in the Garden. Allah reveals this in the Qur'an: **"They will not be affected by any tiredness there..."** (Surat al-Hijr: 48) And in one of the hadith the Messenger of Allah ﷺ tells us that there is no sleep in the Garden:

A man asked the Messenger of Allah ﷺ : "Will the inmates of the Garden sleep?" He replied: "Sleep is the brother of death, and the People of the Garden will not die." (Al-Bayhaqi)

There Will Be No Disagreement:

Among the major attributes of the People of the Garden are their noble qualities of character.

Everyone is comfortable when people have clear consciences and fear Allah. But in a place where such qualities are lacking, people experience opposition, jealousy, touchiness, anger, resentment, mockery and even war. People who are far from the teachings of the Qur'an create an environment with their own hands that resembles Hell. While they could choose to live a life of tolerance, friendship and brotherhood in a comfortable, happy and secure environment, they get caught up in their worldly ambitions, personal passions and desires so that they lose a great blessing. For Muslims, living in this world with awareness, moderation, steadfastness, sensitivity, balance, forgiveness, compassion and love gives a deep, faith-strengthening sense of joy. When a Muslim recognises these fine qualities in himself, it gives him a special joy, he gains a particular pleasure when he sees the same qualities in other Muslims. This timeless pleasure, happiness and beauty grow and increase in the Garden. In one of the hadith, our Prophet ﷺ describes the environment of the Garden:

> *... There will be no disagreement or any hatred amongst them. Their hearts will be as one heart, and they will glorify Allah morning and evening... (Narrated by Abu Hurayra, Sahih Muslim)*

Similar hadith make mention of the character of the people of the Garden:

> *Their character will be according to the character of one man. (Mukhtasar Tadhkirah al-Qurtubi, p. 329/579)*

Similarly, Allah says the following about His faithful slaves whom He finds worthy of the Garden: **"We will strip away any rancour in their hearts – brothers, resting on couches face-to-face"** (Surat al-Hijr: 47) and He tells us of the sincere, heart-felt friendship in which they live.

There Will Be No Sadness or Anxiety:

Those who have no *deen* very often experience the pain of sadness and anxiety. They do not consider that Allah has created everything subject to a decree, and are overwhelmed by fear and panic when they experience adversity or difficulty. Because they do not put their trust in Allah, they become anxious, filled with regret and sadness to such an extent that their health is often damaged. However, a human being does not know what is good or bad for himself; only Allah knows this. This is revealed in a verse of the Qur'an:

… It may be that you hate something when it is good for you and it may be that you love something when it is bad for you. Allah knows and you do not know. (Surat al-Baqara: 216)

What appears to be difficult or worrisome in this world can actually turn into a good thing that will lead one to the Garden. Believers who are aware of this have the ability to keep themselves untouched by things that appear to be difficult or worrisome. The person who subjects himself to Allah and accepts everything He has created is content and at ease. He thinks of everything that happens to him as something good that has come from Allah. In the Garden, by Allah's mercy, he will live far from sadness, worry and other such things. The Prophet ﷺ told us about the maidens of the Garden who say:

We are those who live forever so we do not perish, and we are those who live in ease so we do not live in want and distress, and we are

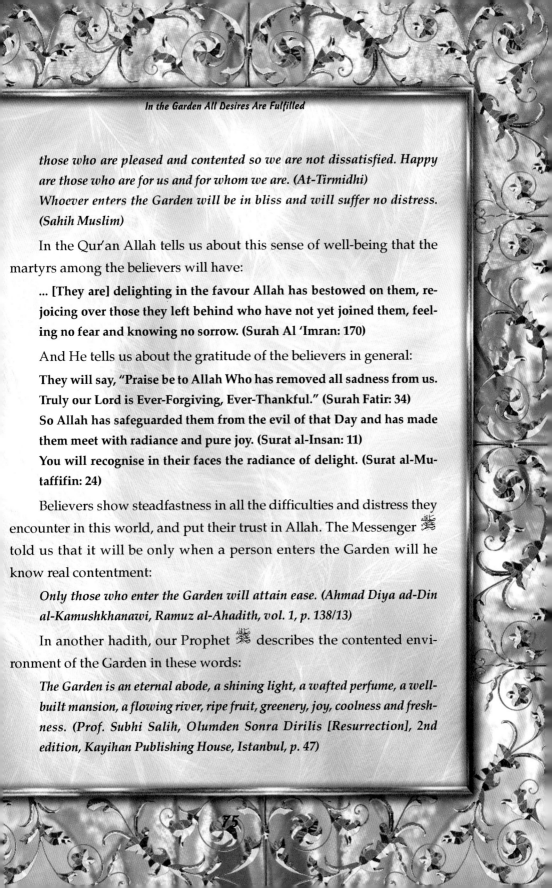

those who are pleased and contented so we are not dissatisfied. Happy are those who are for us and for whom we are. (At-Tirmidhi)

Whoever enters the Garden will be in bliss and will suffer no distress. (Sahih Muslim)

In the Qur'an Allah tells us about this sense of well-being that the martyrs among the believers will have:

... [They are] delighting in the favour Allah has bestowed on them, rejoicing over those they left behind who have not yet joined them, feeling no fear and knowing no sorrow. (Surah Al 'Imran: 170)

And He tells us about the gratitude of the believers in general:

They will say, "Praise be to Allah Who has removed all sadness from us. Truly our Lord is Ever-Forgiving, Ever-Thankful." (Surah Fatir: 34)

So Allah has safeguarded them from the evil of that Day and has made them meet with radiance and pure joy. (Surat al-Insan: 11)

You will recognise in their faces the radiance of delight. (Surat al-Mutaffifin: 24)

Believers show steadfastness in all the difficulties and distress they encounter in this world, and put their trust in Allah. The Messenger ﷺ told us that it will be only when a person enters the Garden will he know real contentment:

Only those who enter the Garden will attain ease. (Ahmad Diya ad-Din al-Kamushkhanawi, Ramuz al-Ahadith, vol. 1, p. 138/13)

In another hadith, our Prophet ﷺ describes the contented environment of the Garden in these words:

The Garden is an eternal abode, a shining light, a wafted perfume, a well-built mansion, a flowing river, ripe fruit, greenery, joy, coolness and freshness. (Prof. Subhi Salih, Olumden Sonra Dirilis [Resurrection], 2nd edition, Kayihan Publishing House, Istanbul, p. 47)

The People of the Garden Are Close to Allah

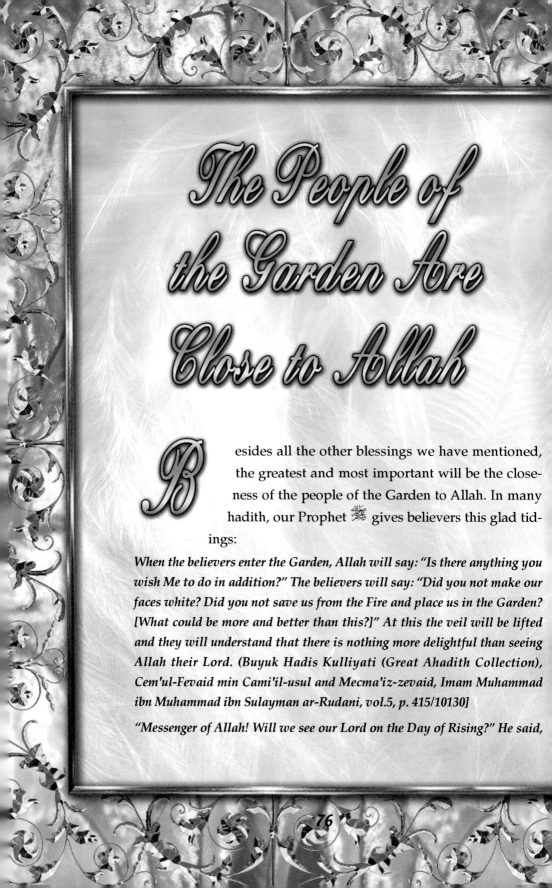

Besides all the other blessings we have mentioned, the greatest and most important will be the closeness of the people of the Garden to Allah. In many hadith, our Prophet ﷺ gives believers this glad tidings:

When the believers enter the Garden, Allah will say: "Is there anything you wish Me to do in addition?" The believers will say: "Did you not make our faces white? Did you not save us from the Fire and place us in the Garden? [What could be more and better than this?]" At this the veil will be lifted and they will understand that there is nothing more delightful than seeing Allah their Lord. (Buyuk Hadis Kulliyati (Great Ahadith Collection), Cem'ul-Fevaid min Cami'il-usul and Mecma'iz-zevaid, Imam Muhammad ibn Muhammad ibn Sulayman ar-Rudani, vol.5, p. 415/10130]

"Messenger of Allah! Will we see our Lord on the Day of Rising?" He said,

"Would you doubt about seeing the moon on the night of the full moon with no screen in between you and it?" They said, "No, Messenger of Allah." He said, "Would you doubt about seeing the sun when there are no clouds between you and it?" They said, "No." He said, "In the same way, you will see Him." (Sahih al-Bukhari; Sahih Muslim; at-Tirmidhi)

Abu Hurayra said, "I said, 'Messenger of Allah, will we see our Lord?' He said, 'Yes. Do you doubt seeing the sun, and the moon on the night when it is full?' We said, 'No.' He said, 'Similarly, you won't doubt seeing your Lord, Mighty is He and Majestic.'" (Sunan Ibn Majah, vol. 5, no.4336)

According to Abu Hurayra, the Prophet 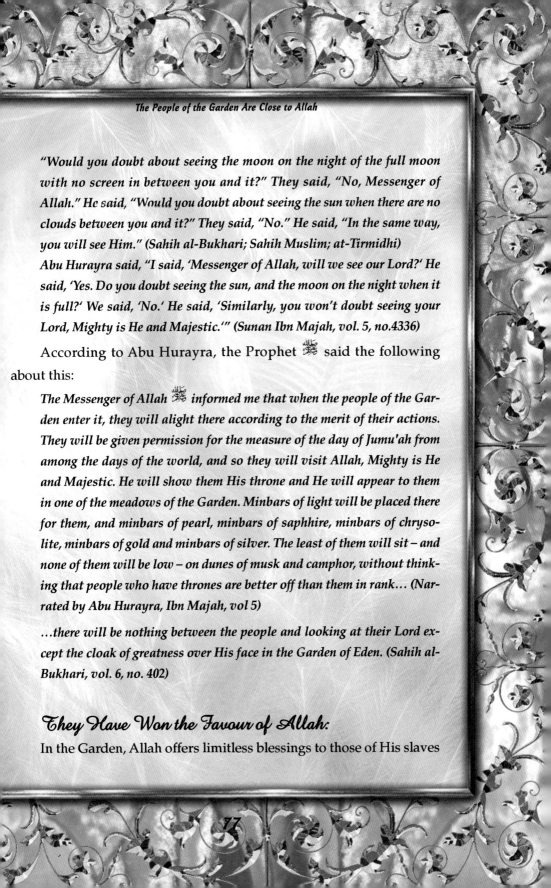 said the following about this:

The Messenger of Allah informed me that when the people of the Garden enter it, they will alight there according to the merit of their actions. They will be given permission for the measure of the day of Jumu'ah from among the days of the world, and so they will visit Allah, Mighty is He and Majestic. He will show them His throne and He will appear to them in one of the meadows of the Garden. Minbars of light will be placed there for them, and minbars of pearl, minbars of saphhire, minbars of chrysolite, minbars of gold and minbars of silver. The least of them will sit – and none of them will be low – on dunes of musk and camphor, without thinking that people who have thrones are better off than them in rank... (Narrated by Abu Hurayra, Ibn Majah, vol 5)

...there will be nothing between the people and looking at their Lord except the cloak of greatness over His face in the Garden of Eden. (Sahih al-Bukhari, vol. 6, no. 402)

They Have Won the Favour of Allah:

In the Garden, Allah offers limitless blessings to those of His slaves who have pleased Him, but above all other blessings, is the fact that they have won Allah's favour. They have given their worldly goods to earn His pleasure and dedicated their lives to Him. In the Garden, they enjoy the pure happiness of having attained their lives' goal. In the Qur'an, Allah tells us what a great blessing it is to earn His favour:

> **Allah has promised the men and women of the muminun Gardens with rivers flowing under them, remaining in them timelessly, for ever, and fine dwellings in the Gardens of Eden. And Allah's good pleasure is even greater. That is the great victory. (Surat at-Tawba: 72)**

Another verse reveals that believers will enjoy every type of happiness in the Garden:

> **O self at rest and at peace, return to your Lord, well-pleasing and well-pleased! Enter among My slaves! Enter My Garden. (Surat al-Fajr: 27-30)**
>
> **Their reward is with their Lord: Gardens of Eden with rivers flowing under them, remaining in them timelessly, for ever and ever. Allah is pleased with them and they are pleased with Him. That is for those who fear their Lord. (Surat al-Bayyina: 8)**

In a hadith we are told that the people of the Garden are pleased in Allah's presence:

> *So they will say, "At Your service, and Your good pleasure, and all good is in Your hands." He will say, "Are you pleased?" They will say, "Why should we not be pleased, Lord, when You have given us that which You have not any others of Your creatures?" He will say, "Should I not give you better than that?" They will say, "Lord, what could be better than that." He will say, "I sanction for you My good pleasure..." (Sahih al-Bukhari)*

The Joy of Having Been Saved from the Fire:

Of course, all the blessings of the Garden are abundant and of great value. There is no place to go in the Hereafter other than the Garden or the Fire. A person who is not accepted into the Garden by Allah will go to the Fire. The existence of the Fire greatly increases the pleasure the people of the Garden derive from it, because not only are they admitted to the Garden but they are also rescued and saved from the Fire.

In this world, Allah alternately shows people good and evil, beauty and ugliness, positive and negative. This is so that people with *deen* can make a comparison and the joy they take in beauty may increase. Some verses of the Qur'an demonstrate that Allah shows the people of the Garden the state of those in the Fire, which may also increase their contentment in the Garden and their joy at being saved from the Fire, and Allah knows best.

The Qur'an reveals the joy that the people of the Garden experience:

> ... They will say, "Praise be to Allah Who has guided us to this! We would not have been guided, had Allah not guided us. The Messengers of our Lord came with the Truth." It will be proclaimed to them: "This is your Garden which you have inherited for what you did." (Surat al-A'raf: 43)

The believers may see the situation of those in the Fire and the sort of reward they have received for what they have done in the world. In the Qur'an, Allah reveals that the people of the Garden speak with the people in the Fire:

> In Gardens they will ask the evildoers: "What caused you to enter Saqar?" They will say, "We were not among those who did the prayer and we did not feed the poor. We plunged with those who plunged and denied the Day of Judgement until the Certain came to us." (Surat al-Muddaththir: 40-47)

The Garden Is from Allah's Justice

Everyone Will Receive the Return for what He Has Done in this World:

In the Qur'an, Allah reveals the purpose of creation:

He Who created death and life to test which of you is best in action… (Surat al-Mulk: 2)

In another verse, we are asked the following:

Did you suppose that We created you for amusement and that you would not return to Us? (Surat al-Muminun: 115)

As long as we are in this world, we are responsible for obeying the Qur'an, seeking Allah's approval in everything we think and do, acting according to the Sunnah of the Messenger of Allah ﷺ, listening to our consciences, living good lives and doing good works. Despite this evident truth, those who live their lives with no regard for the purpose of creation set completely different goals for themselves. However, a record of our works is being kept so that everyone may receive the appropriate reward in the Hereafter for everything he has done and said. Allah, exalted is He, even knows every thought that passes through our minds. As Allah tells us in the Qur'an, everyone will certainly receive the reward for what he has done: **"… You will be questioned about what you did"** (Surat an-Nahl: 93), **"All have ranks according to what they did…"** (Surat al-An'am: 132) However, people of deep knowledge of the deen understand that even if their actions seem good to those who are disbelievers, they are of no use to them as long as they have no iman. Some of the verses in the Qur'an that speak about this matter are as follows:

> **Those the angels take in a virtuous state. They say, "Peace be upon you! Enter the Garden for what you did." (Surat an-Nahl: 32)**
>
> **On the Day that each self finds the good it did, and the evil it did, present there in front of it, it will wish there were an age between it and then… (Surah Al 'Imran: 30)**
>
> **What is with you runs out but what is with Allah goes on for ever. Those who were steadfast will be recompensed according to the best of what they did. Anyone who acts rightly, male or female, being a mumin, We will give them a good life and We will recompense them according to the best of what they did. (Surat an-Nahl: 96-97)**

Allah sees everything that happens; He hears every conversation and whisper; and He knows everything that we do. No secret can be kept from Him. We must be aware that He is at every moment and in every way closer to us than our jugular veins, that He hears every conversation, knows everything that is in our hearts, and sees everything that we do and everything that we see. In the world to come Allah will make it clear that what confronts human beings from Allah will be **"something they did not reckon with."** (Surat az-Zumar: 47) In the world to come, we will receive the reward for everything we have done in public and in solitude, for every word we have uttered, and for things we perhaps thought would remain hidden. This is Allah's eternal justice. This is revealed in the following verse of the Qur'an:

> **Everyone will be ranked according to what they did. We will pay them in full for their actions and they will not be wronged. (Surat al-Ahqaf: 19)**

There Are Ranks in the Garden:

We understand from the Qur'an that people who enter the Garden will be rewarded with a rank corresponding to their submission to Allah.

> **They have different ranks with Allah... (Surah Al 'Imran: 163)**

Of course, no matter what rank a person enjoys in the Garden, he will be content with it because Allah has promised happiness for all His slaves in the Garden. Our Lord has revealed that He will be pleased with His faithful slaves when they enter the Garden and they will be pleased with Him (Surat al-Bayyina: 8). However, just as in this world everyone takes a different pleasure and delight from the same blessings, so in the Garden the degree of pleasure taken from the blessings there may be different. Allah knows best. For example, everyone enjoys looking at a beautiful view but, those whose hearts are closer to Allah and who more greatly appreciate His majesty, may derive greater pleasure from these blessings. In one verse of the Qur'an, Allah describes the qualities of those slaves who will be worthy of high rank:

> **Those who have iman and make hijra and strive in the Way of Allah with their wealth and themselves have a higher rank with Allah. They are the**

They will have in it whatever
they want timelessly,
for ever. It is a binding
promise of your Lord.
(Surat al-Furqan: 116)

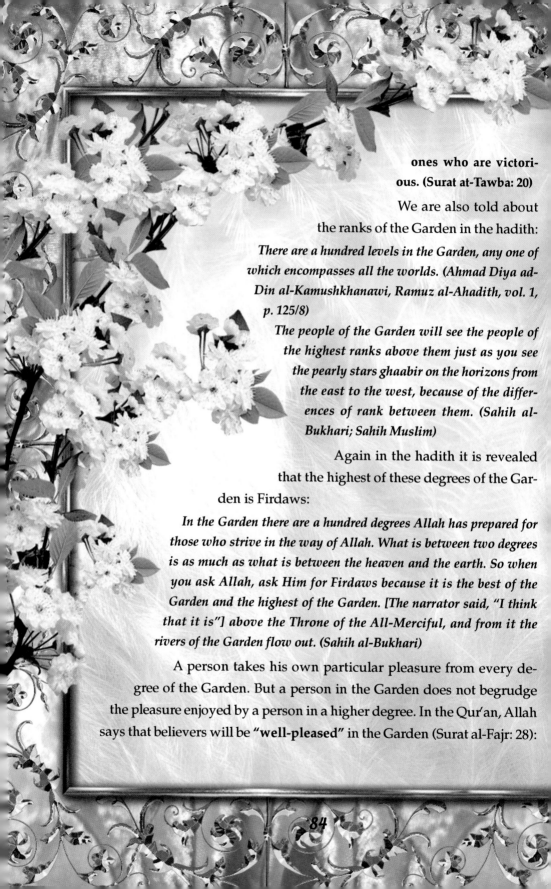

ones who are victorious. (Surat at-Tawba: 20)

We are also told about the ranks of the Garden in the hadith:

There are a hundred levels in the Garden, any one of which encompasses all the worlds. (Ahmad Diya ad-Din al-Kamushkhanawi, Ramuz al-Ahadith, vol. 1, p. 125/8)

The people of the Garden will see the people of the highest ranks above them just as you see the pearly stars ghaabir on the horizons from the east to the west, because of the differences of rank between them. (Sahih al-Bukhari; Sahih Muslim)

Again in the hadith it is revealed that the highest of these degrees of the Garden is Firdaws:

In the Garden there are a hundred degrees Allah has prepared for those who strive in the way of Allah. What is between two degrees is as much as what is between the heaven and the earth. So when you ask Allah, ask Him for Firdaws because it is the best of the Garden and the highest of the Garden. [The narrator said, "I think that it is"] above the Throne of the All-Merciful, and from it the rivers of the Garden flow out. (Sahih al-Bukhari)

A person takes his own particular pleasure from every degree of the Garden. But a person in the Garden does not begrudge the pleasure enjoyed by a person in a higher degree. In the Qur'an, Allah says that believers will be **"well-pleased"** in the Garden (Surat al-Fajr: 28):

"they are pleased with Him" (Surat al-Bayyina: 8) and that they "know no sorrow" there (Surah Al 'Imran: 170). Likewise, another hadith describes the abundance of blessings enjoyed by the People of the Garden in every degree:

> The least of the People of the Garden in rank is the one who will have eighty thousand servants and seventy two wives, and for whom will be set up a dome of pearls, aquamarine and rubies similar in dimensions to the distance between Jabiyah and San'a. (Sunan Ibn Majah; at-Tirmidhi)

The following hadith speaks about the degrees in the Garden:

> The least of the people of the Garden in degree will be the one who gazes at his gardens, his wives, his servants, his couches stretching for the distance travelled in a thousand year. The noblest of them to Allah will be one who gazes on His jamal morning and evening. (Surat al-Qiyama: 21-22) (At-Tirmidhi)

Bediuzzaman Said Nursi said that a person can hope to attain a high degree in the Garden only on the basis of his iman:

> With the light of faith, a person rises to the highest level in the Garden, and assumes a value worthy of the Garden. (Death and Youthfulness, p. 435)

A sincere Muslim must always make effort towards being worthy of the highest rank in Allah's presence in the Garden. A person who has perfected faith and desires above all to be close to Allah is pleasing to Him.

The Qualities of the People of the Garden

Many verses of the Qur'an speak not only of prayer, fasting but also of leading a good life. Allah commands human beings to live good lives themselves and also to counsel others to do the same. In societies that obey the commands of Allah in which everyone leads good lives, a spirit prevails that is similar to that to be found in the life of the Garden.

Muslims are Allah's devoted slaves. They want to please Allah in everything they think, say and do, and they act out of their fear and respect for Him. They never allow themselves to be tempted openly or in secret by any suggestion of Shaytan; they are pure in mind and conscience. And they go into the Hereafter with this clear conscience.

In the Qur'an, Allah reveals the purity of the Muslim's spirit for which He promises them the Garden. He mentions Ibrahim (as) thus:

When he came to his Lord with an unblemished heart. (Surat as-Saffat: 84)

And He mentions the believers thus:

Gardens of Eden with rivers flowing under them, remaining in them timelessly, for ever. That is the reward of those who purify themselves. (Surah Ta Ha: 76)

Sincere Muslims live lives free of greed, grudges, jealousy and other bad qualities and their hearts are bound to Allah. They are people described by Allah in the Qur'an as:

… those who have iman and whose hearts find peace in the remembrance of Allah." (Surat ar-Ra'd: 28)

The glad tidings of the Garden is announced to them:

... for those who have iman and do right actions and humble themselves before their Lord, they are the Companions of the Garden. Remaining in it timelessly, for ever. (Surah Hud: 23)

Elsewhere in the Qur'an Allah says:

O self at rest and at peace, return to your Lord, well-pleasing and well-pleased! Enter among My slaves! Enter My Garden. (Surat al-Fajr: 27-30)

He invites His slaves, being purified in this world and having gained peace of mind, to the Garden.

The thoughts and actions of those who have attained these qualities that please Allah reflect the depth of their faith. Because they act out of their love and fear for Allah, every aspect of their being is good. This goodness comes from their faithful service to Allah. As Allah says in the Qur'an, they are recognised by the mark of prostration on their faces, and of course the mark of prostration is light in the face:

... You see them bowing and prostrating, seeking Allah's good favour and His pleasure. Their mark is on their faces, the traces of prostration. That is their likeness in the Torah. And their likeness in the Injil is that of a seed which puts up a shoot and makes it strong so that it thickens and grows up straight upon its stalk, filling the sowers with delight... (Surat al-Fath: 29)

By Allah's grace, their facial expressions are beautiful and understanding. Their conversations are pleasing to Allah and their words are always edifying. Allah says in the Qur'an that their words always produce good results:

Do you not see how Allah makes a metaphor of a good word: a good tree whose roots are firm and whose branches are in heaven? It bears fruit regularly by its Lord's permission. Allah makes metaphors for people so that hopefully they will pay heed. (Surah Ibrahim: 24-25)

They are obedient, gentle, accommodating, open, sincere and warm. For this reason, they live good lives filled with love and friendship. Allah allows them to experience these blessings in this world, and in the world to come, He will give them endless blessings.

In many hadith, our Prophet ﷺ speaks of the noble qualities of those who enter the Garden, for example:

What are the things that most ensure they enter the Garden? Fear of Allah and noble qualities of character... (Ahmad Diya ad-Din al-Kamushkhanawi, Ramuz al-Ahadith, vol. 1, p.12/8)

Our Prophet ﷺ often reminds us in his hadith that we must "be just," "merciful," "patient," "generous," "pure," "chaste," "honourable" and "truthful."

He also reminds us that, in order to attain the Garden, we must "be benevolent both in private and in public", "speak pleasantly", "praise Allah in broad and narrow straits", "give sadaqah", "seek knowledge", "fear Allah", "obey the Prophets", "refrain from arrogance", "maintain dignity in times of need" and "not resort to begging or shamelessness", "be honest in business", "be at peace in Allah" and "be benevolent for the sake of Allah and the deen".

All these qualities mentioned by our Prophet  are required of Muslims who desire to earn the good pleasure and love of Allah.

Experiencing the Joy of the Garden

One of the greatest blessings for Muslims is the hope they have of attaining the Garden in the Hereafter. Allah created the world so that believers would feel a longing for the Garden. Everyone who believes in Allah and the Last Day will always remember the Garden when experiencing the good things of this world. Knowing that these good things are transitory, they will desire the real and permanent blessings there. So, the longing and enthusiasm of such a person to attain the Garden will be reflected in his behaviour, conversation and his sincere efforts to live a good life.

Because believers long for the Garden, they are always in a state of excitement. And together with their excitement and eagerness, those whom our Lord has made heirs of the incomparable blessings of the Garden live in a state of pleasure and joy as they await the promised Garden.

A person who thinks of the Garden with the intelligence and awareness that comes from faith will live with the awareness of this blessing in the depths of his spirit. In one hadith the Prophet ﷺ tells us that the Garden is more important and valuable than anything else:

And the measure of the bow of any of you or the space of a foot of the Garden is better than the world and everything in it. (Sahih al-Bukhari)
And the measure of the bow of any of you of the Garden will be better than all that over which the sun rises or sets. (Sahih al-Bukhari; Sahih Muslim; at-Tirmidhi)

Throughout this book we have considered descriptions from the Qur'an and the hadith from which we can say that everything pertaining to the Garden is absolutely perfect in itself and when compared with the things of this world. This superiority of the Garden and its perfection are wonderful things for which human beings search this world throughout their whole lives without success. Therefore, to feel a longing for the Garden, to hope to be worthy of it and to experience the joy of our Lord's promise of the Garden are all very great blessings.

Allah is the Only Absolute Being

People who associate His creatures with Allah by attributing power to others apart from Him, unaware that these beings are forms created by Him, will learn in the next world how wrong they have been. Allah tells us in the Qur'an that those who put other things in His place will see these things disappear.

See how they lie against themselves and how what they invented has forsaken them! (Surat al-An'am: 24)

... "Where are those you called upon besides Allah?" They will say, "They have forsaken us"... (Surat al-A'raf: 37)

... They have lost their own selves and what they invented has forsaken them. (Surat al-A'raf: 53)

... They will be returned to Allah, their Master, the Real, and what they invented will abandon them. (Surah Yunus: 30)

Then they will be asked, "Where are those besides Allah you associated with Him?" and they will reply, "They have forsaken us. Or rather we were not calling to anything at all before." That is how Allah misguides the kafirun. (Surah Ghafir: 74)

As Allah says in the verse from Surah Ghafir, when these people die, they will understand that what they had worshipped in this world was an image. They may then say "we were not calling to anything at all before" but those with intelligence and awareness must consider and understand this truth which everyone will fully understand in the world to come, in this world while there is still time.

Conclusion

All the wonderful things we have related in this book are as near to us as the very next instant. The life of this world may come to an end at any time, and this will be the beginning of endless life in the world to come. Therefore it is very important for us to realise that the next life may come at any second; we must all fear the possibility of going to the Fire and prepare ourselves in order to attain the endless blessing of the Garden.

But Shaytan wants us to forget the wonderful things that Allah has promised in the Garden; he wants us to be heedless and not think about eternal life. On the contrary, he shows us how to be content with the flawed blessings found in this world and insinuates that we will benefit by being contented with these blessings for a few decades. But it is necessary for us to act contrary to Shaytan's insinuations, and to persevere in sincerity and keep in mind that both the Fire and the Garden are very near.

All sincere Muslims trust in the endless mercy, and in the limitless intelligence and power of Allah. We trust that He loves us, protects us, desires our good in this world and the next, and wants a good and honourable life for us in this world and the Garden in the world to come. Therefore, we must never forget this joyous blessing, and we must spread the glad tidings among ourselves of this blessing soon to come. In the Qur'an, Allah commands believers to share this good news:

> Allah has bought from the muminun their selves and their wealth in return for the Garden. They fight in the Way of Allah and they kill and are killed. It is a promise binding on Him in the Torah, the Injil and the Qur'an. And who is truer to his contract than Allah? Rejoice then in the bargain you have made. That is the great victory. (Surat at-Tawba: 111)

They said, "Glory be to You!
We have no knowledge except
what You have taught us.
You are the All-Knowing,
the All-Wise."

(Surat al-Baqara: 32)